Instructor's
Media Planning Workbook

MW01141418

William B. Goodrich
Jack Z. Sissors

FIFTH EDITION

William B. Goodrich
University of South Carolina

Jack Z. Sissors
Northwestern University

Printed on recyclable paper

NTC Business Books
a division of *NTC Publishing Group* • Lincolnwood, Illinois USA

6 7 8 9 ML 0 9 8 7 6 5 4 3 2 1

Contents

Section Three   Media Strategy Planning Problems

Section Four   Miscellaneous Problems

Introduction

This instructor's manual has been designed to help you and your students get the most out of the *Media Planning Workbook*. Media planning problems often do not have a single, clear-cut answer. The same set of facts can be interpreted differently by different planners. It is important that you keep this in mind when grading assignments. You might find that students' solutions differ from those given in this manual. Their solutions can be acceptable alternatives, provided they give valid reasons to justify the answer. Where appropriate, stress to students the importance of explaining the reasons for their solutions.

A number of the assignments deal with developing reach and frequency estimates for various media. In calculating the answers, it is often necessary to round some numbers as you proceed through the problem. As a result, students might develop a final answer that is slightly different from the ones printed in this manual. It is recommended that answers that fall within a point of the reach percentage or one-tenth of a point of the frequency be considered correct. After all, we are dealing with estimates, not exact values.

We recommend that you review the solutions to each problem before making the assignment. In addition to the solutions, this manual contains suggestions on how to use each assignment and what to emphasize in class.

The "How to Use This Assignment" section has been included because the authors' experiences with the assignments have indicated that some work better as in-class discussions rather than as take-home assignments. Experience with the assignments has also indicated areas in which students often have difficulty in understanding the concept of the necessary mathematical calculations. These areas are covered in the "What to Emphasize in Class" section of the solutions to each assignment.

W. B. G.
J. Z. S.

Section One

Marketing Analysis Problems

Using Demographic and Index Numbers

How to Use This Assignment

This assignment is an introduction to data, including index numbers, that are to be used primarily to define target audiences of media vehicles. Because index numbers are also used in many other marketing and advertising analyses, the broad scope of index numbers should be mentioned.

It is suggested that the instructor start with an explanation of what media planners want to know, and then show how Simmons and MRI provide the answers through data that contribute to the solution of media problems. However, the focus of attention should be on the meaning and use of the different types of percentages and index numbers.

There are a number of ways to attain this goal. Some students can quickly grasp the concept with one explanation. Others will require repeated explanations. It usually helps if students know the two methods of calculating index numbers, as explained in the fifth edition of *Advertising Media Planning*. Sometimes students catch on after they have learned how to calculate the numbers. One major problem with some students who have difficulty learning the meaning of index numbers and percentages is that they are weak on mathematical relationships of all kinds. Perhaps some students never understood the meaning of percentages back in the fifth or sixth grade.

For those who have trouble understanding percentages, it might be necessary to have them read an elementary math book and learn to solve the problems there before proceeding to index numbers.

What to Emphasize in Class

Even when students are quite competent in the use of percentages, they are somewhat confused by cross-tabulated percentages such as found in Simmons, MRI, and much marketing research data. Therefore, students' attention should be called to the whole concept of cross-tabulations. Note that a percentage from column B cannot be added to one in column C.

Another part of cross-tabulated percentages that students should know is that the basis for each percentage is different. Emphasis should be concentrated on where each percentage base is located and what each base means. Here is an example taken from Exhibit 1–1:

> The number of gelatin/gelatin desserts users shown in the "All" users column for ages 18–24 is 2,502. There are two different bases used to calculate the percentages for columns B and C, but they are sometimes easily confused. So urge students to know precisely how these bases differ as follows:

	Percentage of whom?	Percent	Base number	Base
Column B:	Female homemaker users aged 18–24 as a percent of all female homemaker users	6.6	37,750	All users
Column C:	Percentage of all female homemakers aged 18–24 who are users	33.2	7,537	All female homemakers aged 18–24

In other words, column B shows the importance of the demographic group as a percentage of all users, and column C shows the intensity of usage within the demographic group.

Ask students to calculate each of the two percentages shown above as follows:

Column B: $\dfrac{2,502}{37,750} = .6627$ or 6.6%   Column C: $\dfrac{2,502}{7,537} = .3319$ or 33.2%

The instructor should remind students *always* to ask, "What is this a percentage of? (What base?)" whenever they see a percentage. Once they understand the meaning of percentages, then they are likely to understand the relationships shown by index numbers.

One final thing to emphasize is the fact that percentages and index numbers calculated on very small bases are not as meaningful as those calculated from large bases. If a student should read that 50 percent of consumers used a product, it would make a great deal of difference if the base were 20 or 20,000. One should not generalize from statistical data that come from small bases.

Answers to Problems for Assignment 1

1. 15.6% (Column B)

2. 38.1% (Column B)

3. 18,425,000 (Total U.S. column)

4. 910,000 (Column A)

5. 22.1% (Column C)

6. 16.5% (Column C)

7. More likely (Column D) (Index is above 100)

8. 48% (Column D) (148−100 = 48)

9. 30,750,000 (Total U.S. Column−Column A) (52,912−22,162 = 30,750)

10. They total over 100 percent because the demographic segments are not mutually exclusive. In other words, a user could have several children and be counted in more than one of the groups. This duplication results in totals higher than 100 percent.

Misleading Index Numbers

How to Use This Assignment

This assignment is appropriate for in-class discussion, as it requires review of just a few numbers and calls for alertness to misuse of data. You could divide the class into small groups for discussion to see if each group reaches the same conclusions. It might be best to ask students to determine the proper use of index numbers in this assignment *before* you underline the specific lessons to be learned in this assignment.

The key points to emphasize will seem more relevant after the students have had the opportunity to analyze the problems given in this assignment.

What to Emphasize in Class

The simple, but important, points that are emphasized by this assignment are (indexed to question):

1. Do not ignore size of demographic or geographic segment. Do not select the highest index when it represents a small market segment (unless some unique market situation prompts you to ignore this axiom, which is almost always valid).

2. a. If budget permits, a large or otherwise potentially important market probably should not be totally ignored—even if the market has a relatively low index number. (Of course, if usage is virtually nonexistent, like snow tires in Miami, the market should be ignored no matter how large the market segment.)

    Large metropolitan markets are generally considered important because of reasons such as total potential volume, need to support central city and outlying distribution, higher media coverage levels, more efficient media delivery, greater sales force, and competitive pressures.

    b. Smaller, but high-use, markets can be important, especially if budget is limited or if the planner is adding further media effort beyond the basic amount required to maintain basic distribution and consumer acceptance levels.

Answers to Problems for Assignment 2

The following are suggested solutions and key points that should be considered for each question in this assignment.

1. It is assumed that the usage index numbers are basically comparable for the three largest geographic regions. Therefore, the least complicated solution is to consider the amount of total sales available in each region.

Rank	Region	Data used	Explanation
1	C	36.8% volume	Rank order of volume accounted for
2	B	29.9% volume	in each of the four regions
3	A	25.5% volume	
4	D	7.8% volume	

However, it should be noted that there can be situations where the ranking would be different:

Possible rankings	Region	Data used	Explanation
1,2,3	A	105 index	Represents slightly higher consumption per thousand targets available to be reached than B or C
1 or 2	B	29.9% volume	Represents total volume almost at the level of the largest region with slightly higher consumption per thousand targets reached
1,2,3	C	36.8% volume	Would seem too large to ignore (and usage index only slightly lower than average)
1 or 4	D	110 index	If used as test market or first part of roll-out, this market could be considered the first region used due to lower amount of investment risk and slightly greater levels of general product acceptance. However, this market region would probably be considered too small for sole long-term investment, unless only a quite limited geographic effort is affordable.

Of course, distribution, sales, and other marketing efforts or factors for other products marketed by the company, as well as various competitive considerations, can be major determinants in regional selection. Further, geographic location of regions relative to each other is important, because various barriers might isolate one or more regions.

2. a. The answer (a quite common one in advertising) is that it all depends on the situation. Admittedly, an index of 54, when compared with an index of 127 or 164, is relatively weak. However, for various reasons it is unwise to ignore a market large enough to account for 6.7 percent of total U.S. population. Considerable analysis and a top management decision would be needed to ignore such a large market.

   If available budget calls for considerably less than full national coverage, and if it seems unlikely that adequate sales and profits can be generated for the investment needed for such an effort in a major market (such as market A in this instance), it is quite reasonable to drop such a market. If the required investment can be placed to better advantage in other markets, this would further argue for switching of funds from market A to other, more potentially profitable, markets.

A final point that should be raised is whether the "usage index" refers to total product category usage or specific brand usage. If this low index (54) represents development of the total category (CDI), it would indicate that consumers in this market use less of this type of product. If this index represents usage or development of brand consumption (BDI), it is possible that CDI could be high and indicate high future growth potential for this brand in this major market. However, it is important to determine why product usage is low before arbitrarily deciding to place advertising in the market.

2. b. Volume and profit potential per advertising impression or dollar spent will probably be highest in the three smallest markets. If all markets have received a basic level of advertising (say, enough to maintain distribution and consumer awareness), a heavy-up effort in the three smaller markets (B,C, and D) will reach more users than exist in the largest market (A). Purchase of adequate media impressions to reach a reasonable number of the 6.7 percent of population in market A would only match against 3.6 percent of product volume. On the other hand, covering the total of 5.7 percent of population in the smaller three markets would match against 6.9 percent of volume (almost twice as much volume as exists in market A).

Comments

Understanding the concepts and reasoning used to reach the recommended solutions is most important. Although the given solutions are believed the best solutions, it is possible for the student to answer the questions differently based on certain assumptions that also make sense. Examples of such assumptions are given with the stated solutions.

These examples (which are presented out of context for an actual market problem) might seem overly simplistic to students. It can be helpful to look for comparable situations in "real world" marketing media problems. Such problems would probably present a more realistic marketing situation, including a more complete and extensive list of markets to be reached within a given budget. The problem included in Assignment 9 in this workbook provides a more detailed market selection simulation that is a logical follow-up to this assignment.

The major purpose of this assignment is to make students aware of possible "quick conclusions" that under further analysis clearly become inappropriate for the marketing situation.

Using Simmons for Selecting Primary Target Demographics

How to Use This Assignment

The student will find this assignment easiest when it is used with or immediately following the first two assignments on demographic data and index numbers. Students can turn in their answers or discuss in class.

What to Emphasize in Class

Review with students how to compute the missing data asked for in Problem 1 of this assignment. The purpose of this assignment is to make students familiar with the Simmons format of presenting usage data. This assignment again gives you the opportunity to point out major considerations for determining which are the key demographic segments. The students should review the data in terms of total users and heavy users. They should also consider the size of the demographic segment, as well as index numbers.

You can also point out that in their printed data Simmons often omits medium and light usage data to cut down on the size of the reports. This is why those data are missing from Exhibit 3–1. Medium and light usage data is available to subscribers via online computer access.

Answers to Problems for Assignment 3

1. Demographic group	Column B %	Column C %	Index
Adults aged 18–24	7.5	7.1	100
25–34	23.9	7.6	107
35–44	23.1	7.1	100
45–54	9.3	4.0	56
55–64	15.4	9.0	127
65 or older	20.8	7.9	111

For the 25–34 segment, the numbers are calculated as follows:

$$\text{Column B} = \frac{1{,}968}{8{,}223} = .2393 \text{ or } 23.9\%$$

$$\text{Column C} = \frac{1{,}968}{25{,}859} = .0761 \text{ or } 7.6\%$$

$$\text{Index} = \frac{7.6}{7.1} \times 100 = 107$$

		Heavy users	
2. Rank	Demographic age segment	Number (000)	Index
1	25–34	4,617	119
2	35–44	4,496	118
3	45–54	3,482	128*
4	18–24	1,820	81
5	55–64	1,654	83*
6	65 or older	1,524	52

*Students might rank the 45–54 age group in first place because of the large index number (128) for that group. Also, they might rank the 55–64 age group in fourth place because it has a slightly higher index number than the 18–24 age group. This provides a good discussion point on which many marketers disagree. Some think that the size of the group should be the determining factor, and others think high incidence of usage (index number) should decide the ranking. The authors ranked the 45–54 group third because the size of the group is 20–25 percent smaller than either of the first two groups, and the first two groups also have above-average index numbers. Fourth and fifth places were based on the sizes of the groups because the index numbers are almost the same.

3. The larger the household, the more likely they are to be heavy users of diet or sugar free cola drinks. Conversely, households of only one or two persons are less likely to be heavy users of the product.

   The same holds true for households with children. Heavy users of diet or sugar free cola drinks are in households with children. Households with no children are 16 percent less likely to be heavy users.

4. Usage of diet or sugar free cola drinks increases with household income. Households with incomes of $30,000 or more are above average in usage, and households earning less than $30,000 are below average.

Analyzing Product Usage Data of Media Audiences

How to Use This Assignment

This assignment can be used for class discussion or as a written assignment. The key to completing this assignment is to understand what the numbers mean in the MRI and Simmons exhibits discussed in earlier assignments.

What to Emphasize in Class

This assignment provides an opportunity to discuss the values of employing product usage information provided for various media. This type of analysis can be compared with the process of selecting primary demographic targets and matching media audiences against selected key demographics.

It should be emphasized that, in addition to the questions raised in this assignment, many other factors must be considered when a planner selects specific media vehicles to deliver advertising messages to the best prospects. The purpose of this assignment is to review one type of analysis available to media planners and to make students familiar with this type of data and what it means. Of course, various other factors have been assumed to simplify the questions.

Questions 2 and 4 call for an understanding of what is meant by CPM (discussed later in Assignment 12). Students might think that the magazines or TV programs delivering the largest number of heavy users will be the most cost efficient. However, if CPM total audience is the same for each magazine or TV program, then those with the highest proportion of heavy users (percentage of total audience who are heavy users) will be the ones that deliver heavy users most efficiently. While high heavy user index numbers are the key to the solution, you might want to ask students to compute the percentage of heavy users represented in the total audience of each vehicle selected.

Answers to Problems for Assignment 4

	Publication	Number of heavy users reached	Heavy users reached (%)
1.	*BHG/LHJ Combo*	8,589,000	47.4
	Family Circle/McCall's	8,539,000	47.1
	Parade	7,772,000	42.9

2. Publication	Number of heavy users reached	Heavy users reached (%)	Heavy user index*	Heavy users as % of total audience*
WWF Magazine	183,000	1.0	168	35.6
Seventeen	1,100,000	6.1	155	32.9
Golf Illustrated	200,000	1.1	151	32.2

*Although not asked for in the answer, these data are the basis for selecting the publications. You might want to request that students provide the index numbers and column C percentages for the publications selected.

3. Radio Network	Number of users reached	Users reached (%)
Internet	33,379,000	43.1
Katz Radio Group	29,972,000	38.7
ABC Prime	14,419,000	18.6

4. Radio Network	Number of heavy users reached	Heavy users reached (%)	Heavy user index*	Heavy users as % of total audience*
STRZ Entertainment	375,000	2.1	141	29.9
AURN	535,000	3.0	129	27.3
Power	1,218,000	6.7	116	24.6

*Although not asked for in the answer, these data are the basis for selecting the networks. You might want to request that students provide index numbers and column C percentages for the networks selected.

5. Pvt. Det/Susp/Myst/Pol.—Prime   3,117,000 heavy users/17.2% reach

6. CNN (Cable News Network)   26,117,000 users/33.7% reach

Analyzing Market Data

How to Use This Assignment

This assignment should come early in the course, at the time you are lecturing on marketing or marketing analysis. It can be used either as a take-home exercise or as part of a lecture. The only advantage in having students take it home is that they will have more time to work with it. On the other hand, if the assignment is used during a class session, the instructor can provide hints on how to best interpret the data.

What to Emphasize in Class

Emphasize the fact that media planners need to know as much about the marketplace as possible, even though some pieces of information cannot be directly used in planning media.

Also, emphasize the necessity for doing additional calculations of marketing data that could help the student better understand their impact. For example, the student should calculate index numbers for at least 1992 and 1995 for each of the six bimonthly periods, to learn whether consumers changed their seasonal purchasing habits between 1992 and 1995. Also, students should calculate the percentage of money spent by brand A in each of the bimonthly periods, etc.

Call attention to the fact that often the brand with the largest market share also has the largest distribution nationally. Also call attention to the fact that some brands seem to spend more money on sales promotion, rather than on regular advertising.

Finally, emphasize the necessity for making assumptions about missing data. Media and marketing planners rarely have all the data they want. They therefore make assumptions about how the marketplace is operating and try to challenge their assumptions as time goes on, correcting whatever was found to be wrong originally.

Answer to Problem for Assignment 5

Following is a list of facts gleaned from the data, presented in outline form for convenience. After each fact is an estimate of how this information might be used in marketing and media planning. Urge students to find ways to make the information useful.

This market is growing, albeit at an uneven pace. Industry sales grew 9.8 percent from 1992 to 1993, grew only 1.0 percent from 1993 to 1994, and grew 6.9 percent from 1994 to 1995. It would help to have known the kind of product market it is as a means of explaining the growth. This was not given, so the next question might be: Did the growth keep up with population, or was it growing at a different rate than population? Expanding markets with great opportunity usually grow faster than the population grows.

In any case, this information provides perspective for studying a brand. If brands grow faster than the category as a whole, this could be helpful in planning strategy. Probably a larger advertising budget would be justified.

Finally, this is the kind of auxiliary information that helps a planner indirectly in making decisions about other things.

Winter months are above average in sales. The value of knowing this is obvious for media planning. The principle is to advertise when sales are going well. In this situation, the category shows sales in every month of the year, but with greater sales in winter, suggesting that advertising be done all year round, but with a heavy-up in winter.

There is not much change in bimonthly sales patterns from 1992 to 1995. The data suggest that consumers tend to buy at certain times of the year and that this pattern has not changed much. Students should have indexed the six bimonthly periods for 1992 and 1995 and have confirmed the consistent sales pattern.

Brand A has the largest share of market and has improved its position slightly over the years. In planning media for any other competitor, the student should keep brand A's marketing and media strategy in mind because of its strong leadership position. This is especially important if a planner wants to steal customers from other brands. The student might not want to plan media exactly as brand A does, but the brand cannot be ignored in this media plan.

Brand B has a much smaller market share than A, and its share has eroded over the years. The student should want to know why this is happening. Is brand B's product inferior? It is known to have less distribution than A, but it has more distribution than C. Yet C has shown some growth.

The student should note that "all other" brands' shares are fairly stable after 1993 and even show some growth. Is brand B losing customers to private or smaller national brands?

Despite the fact that sales vary a great deal in the winter (from the first table), brand A maintains its leadership position in each month of the year. Also, brand A seems to do even better against competitors in the warm months (May, June, July, and August). Students should ask for possible assumptions to explain this phenomenon. One possible reason is that competitors might not advertise much in summer months, while brand A does. Therefore, it does better in the summer months. Data from the media expenditure chart provide some substantiation, although not completely.

Brand A has by far the largest percentage of national distribution. It is so large (97 percent) that it suggests that the company does a great deal of national advertising to support it. The expenditure chart supports that point of view; 87 percent of Brand A's budget goes into network television.

Most of brand A's money goes into television (97 percent spot and network TV). Brand A's media strategy is based on using a medium that has sight and sound. Competitors with a good message and an equally good product might also want to use television heavily. But competitors with undifferentiated products and messages would want to use other media.

Ten percent of Brand A's budget goes into spot TV. This suggests that perhaps there are a number of markets with good potential that need heavying-up. Or perhaps network ratings are low in some good markets and more gross rating points are needed to bring these markets up to average.

Brand A spends the largest percentage of advertising dollars in September–October. It also spends its largest percentage of promotional dollars in the same two-month period. This suggests that brand A wants to start spending heavily a bit before there are large increases in category sales, perhaps to get the jump on competitors.

Brand A uses both advertising and sales promotion dollars to sell its product. This is a double-barreled approach to selling and suggests that each marketing element has a specific task to accomplish (although the student cannot know what it is from the limited data).

Brand C spends a larger proportion of its volume in sales promotion offers than the other two brands. Perhaps brand C sells exclusively through sales promotion. Of course it might use media, but only to announce the deals—not to sell in the same manner as brand A.

Brand A spends a smaller proportion of its money in November–December than it does in September–October, even though category sales are highest in the last two months. This suggests (but does not prove) that perhaps the product is the kind that is not exciting when compared to the other products advertised in the Christmas season. We know that some companies even pull all their advertising out of December because of this problem. Perhaps this is one of those situations.

Using Sales & Marketing Management Survey of Buying Power Data

How to Use This Assignment

Because this assignment requires a number of mathematical calculations, it seems best to use it as a take-home assignment. When completed, the assignment can be discussed in class prior to handing it in for grading.

What to Emphasize in Class

Review with students the method for creating a multiple-factor index discussed in the workbook. Remind students that when creating an index as called for in this assignment, it is possible to add numbers that represent unlike measurements. Using the three-factor index example in this assignment, point out how the market value index was derived and how this determined the budget allocation.

It is suggested that you show how the dollar figures for Effective Buying Income (EBI) and retail sales are rounded in developing the index so that they will not be so large as to minimize the influence of the lower population numbers. For example, you might develop in class the population, EBI, and retail sales numbers for the first market in the assignment—Cedar Rapids. Explain that the population figure, 174.7, is taken directly from Exhibit 6–1 in the workbook. However, the EBI figure of 3,056,653 is rounded to 3,056.7, and the Eating and Drinking Places figure of 192,598 is rounded to 192.6.

You might also want to point out to students that in the workbook exhibit and assignment, only small differences result from computing the value index rather than using a single item such as population or sales by store group. However, it often does make a difference as can be seen when the data for Sioux City and Waterloo–Cedar Falls are compared. The market list would have been different if only population was used as a single factor for selection. And even small differences can be important when large budgets are involved.

Answer to Problem for Assignment 6

The table below shows the correct answer to this assignment. Note that the selected markets are the only ones for which the budget has been allocated. You might want to have your students submit their solutions to this assignment in the format in which our solution is shown, as this will facilitate grading.

Market	Population (000)	EBI (000,000)	Eating and drinking places (000,000)	Sum of factors	Market value index (%)	Budget allocation
Cedar Rapids	174.7	3,056.7	192.6	3,424.0[a]	17.4	$ 69,600
Davenport–Moline–Rock Island	353.3	5,327.5	356.5	6,037.3[a]	30.7	122,800
Des Moines	414.8	7,401.2	426.1	8,242.1[a]	41.9	167,600
Dubuque	87.3	1,242.7	87.6	1,417.6		
Iowa City	100.6	1,724.9	109.4	1,934.9		
Sioux City	118.4	1,747.3	114.7	1,980.4[a]	10.0[b]	40,000
Waterloo–Cedar Falls	124.1	1,741.5	107.3	1,972.9		
				19,683.8[a]	100.0	$400,000

[a]Top four markets chosen; total sum of factors for chosen markets only.
[b]Rounded down from 10.1 to 10.0 to stay within budget.

Additional Assignments

The data in Exhibit 6–1 provide the opportunity for a number of other assignments and for in-class discussions. Some suggestions follow:

- Develop a multiple-factor index for different types of products that will require using different retail sales data, e.g., a new dessert mix (food store/supermarket sales), a new hair coloring (drug), or a new line of compact appliances (furniture/home furnishings/appliances).

- Provide demographic data on a product and use them to modify the population and EBI data. For example, suppose the product's target audience is adults aged 35–49 with incomes over $55,000. Show how population and EBI data could be modified based on the information given in Exhibit 6–1.

- Discuss the problem of weighting factors. Consider a product that is sold through several types of outlets, e.g., food stores and drugstores. Assuming that sales are 60 percent food and 40 percent drug, show how the buying power data could be weighted.

- Alter the total budget and/or number of markets.

Competitive Media Expenditure Analysis

How to Use This Assignment

The data provided in Exhibit 7–1 can form the basis for a class discussion of media expenditure data. However, the assignment itself will probably work best as a homework assignment, due to the calculations needed. When the assignments are given back to the students, you have a fine opportunity to discuss media opportunities.

What to Emphasize in Class

Most students would benefit from a review of how to compute percentage change. Also, explain the need to look for "opportunities." An opportunity represents some area that the competition has not exploited for one reason or another. This is brought out in the suggested solution to question 4.

Answers to Problems for Assignment 7

1.

	1993 ($000)	1994 ($000)	Percentage Change Y/A
Sealy	$22,799.8	$29,851.6	31%
Select Comfort	3,237.8	4,896.7	51
Serta	7,599.1	9,091.2	20
Simmons	6,714.7	7,716.0	15
Sleepys	4,457.6	5,556.9	25
Spring Air	1,133.6	1,110.0	−2

2. Sealy spent 84 percent of their total budget in the first six months of the year. Serta spent heavily (97 percent of the total budget) in the first and third quarters of the year and little the rest of the year. Simmons spent relatively little (3 percent) in the first quarter and emphasized the second (34 percent) and third (45 percent) quarters.

3.

			Sunday			Network	Spot	Syndicated	Cable	Network	Spot
Brand	Total	Magazines	Magazines	Newspapers	Outdoor	TV	TV	TV	TV	Radio	Radio
Sealy	$29,851.6	$ 316.4	$223.6	$ 188.1	—	$17,222.3	$2,635.8	$7,043.0	$2,222.4	—	—
% of brand total		1.1	.7	.6		57.7	8.8	23.6	7.4		
Select	4,896.7	4,587.7	27.8	68.0	6.6	—	30.1	120.8	24.1	31.6	—
% of brand total		93.7	.6	1.4	.1		.6	2.5	.5	.6	
Serta	9,091.2	—	—	27.2	26.4	7,389.5	605.4	—	1,042.7	—	—
% of brand total				.3	.3	81.3	6.6		11.5		
Simmons	7,716.0	4,368.1	—	197.9	—	—	2,438.6	—	711.4	—	—
% of brand total		56.6		2.6			31.6		9.2		
Sleepys	5,556.9	—	—	5,556.9	—	—	—	—	—	—	—
% of brand total				100.0							
Spring Air	1,110.0	35.2	—	—	—	275.4	86.6	—	398.8	311.5	2.5
% of brand total		3.2				24.8	7.8		35.9	28.1	.2
Six brand total	58,222.4	9,307.4	251.4	6,038.1	33.0	24,887.2	5,796.5	7,163.8	4,399.4	343.1	2.5
% of six brand total		16.0	.4	10.4	.1	42.7	10.0	12.3	7.5	.6	<.1

($000)

4. Special consideration should be given to media classes that are lightly (or not) used by the competition. If the media classes are compatible with the creative platform for your brand, they will provide your brand with the opportunity to out-advertise the competition in those particular media.

Magazines. A possibility, but it would be hard to dominate in magazines, given the major expenditures by Select and Simmons. Further investigation about the types of magazines being used might provide insights into opportunities in this class.

Sunday magazines. A possible print choice, because very little use is being made of this media class, and it can provide national coverage and good color reproduction. However, the cost is high, and it would have to be used sparingly, perhaps just in selected key markets.

Newspapers. Might be used as part of a co-op effort with local dealers. Would not be practical for your national effort.

Outdoor. Although little used, it might not be appropriate for a national launch, considering the short message length. Might be used as a supplemental medium if it does not divert too many dollars from other media classes.

Network TV. Seems a poor choice given a limited budget and the heavy use made by Sealy and Serta. Perhaps network TV use in the fourth quarter could be justified, because both Sealy and Serta are light advertisers in that quarter.

Spot TV. A possibility for local market heavy-up if needed. Further investigation of which spot TV markets are being used by competitors could uncover some opportunities.

Syndicated TV. A possibility, but your brand's modest budget will not permit a very aggressive posture even in syndicated TV. If needed, it might be used for seasonal heavy-up.

Cable TV. A good possibility because you can target your messages to a carefully selected audience. Cable TV also allows you to have a presence in television at a reasonable cost.

Network radio. A good possibility because the class is underused by the competition. Selection of radio would depend in part on the creative platform for the brand. If the media class is compatible with the brand's creative message, this could be a good way to achieve low-cost national coverage.

Spot radio. A good possibility if a spot market effort is desirable. A strong spot radio campaign could get more mileage for the brand than going head to head with competitors in spot TV.

Note that although a number of media choices could be justified, the student's rationale supporting his or her choices is more important than the actual choices. Encourage students to explain why they selected the media classes they did.

5. Sleepys advertising has run exclusively in newspapers; no national media were used. Considering the significant budget size (over $5.5 million), Sleepys is most likely a regional brand.

Using SRDS Media Information

How to Use This Assignment

This assignment deals with the extraction of information from SRDS. It can be used as a take-home assignment, but it works just as well as an in-class assignment. Because all students have the same source material, they can all see how the information was found and where to look for data in SRDS.

What to Emphasize in Class

You should make the point that SRDS follows the same basic format for all entries in each volume. Although *McCall's* is only one example, the same format is followed for all magazines (e.g., item 5 is always the black/white rates, item 16 is always issue and closing dates).

Some specific details to point out include the following:

- Costs for regional editions of a magazine are often figured on CPM circulation (Exhibit 8–1, 13a—"Geographic and/or Demographic Editions").

- Magazine covers are more expensive than inside pages (Exhibit 8–1, 7).

- Publishers offer different types of discounts: volume, seasonal, consecutive page.

- Standard advertising units (SAU) provide standardized newspaper ad sizes for national advertisers. Most newspapers now charge national advertisers by the inch, just as they do for local advertisers.

- Newspaper rate and discount structures include open rate, bulk contract rates, and contract year.

- Trade magazines provide "Territorial Distribution" and "Business Analysis of Circulation" (Exhibit 8–3, 18). Junior pages apply to tabloid-size magazines (Exhibit 8–3, items 5 and 15 under *Gourmet News*). Finally, small space ads can be used as rate holders to earn lower rates by increasing the frequency of insertions.

- If you have not yet used Assignment 12 on cost-per-thousand (CPM) concepts, you should go over the method used to compute CPM, because question 6 of this assignment requires such computations.

Answers to Problems for Assignment 8

1. $543,384.30. All ads receive the 10 percent volume discount, and the ads run in January and July receive an additional 7 percent seasonal discount. $(6 \times 103,305 \times .90) - (2 \times 103,305 \times .07) = 557,847 - 14,462.70 = 543,384.30$. See Exhibit 8–1, 5—Volume Discount and Seasonal Discount.

2. 1,426,000 (550,000 + 876,000)
   $22.55
   $32,156.30 ([550 + 876] × 22.55 = 32,156.30)

3. 10/14
   3/7

4. $123,263.30 ($148,510 less the 10 percent volume and 7 percent seasonal discounts)

5. 546 (10.5 inches × 4 columns × 13 insertions)

6. *Denver Post* $17.73
   Rocky Mountain News $19.41
   To compute CPM for the *Denver Post,* first figure the ad cost: 500″ rate of $124.00 per inch times 42 inches (10.5″ × 4 columns) = $5,208.00. Next, divide the total daily circulation by 1,000 (293,777 ÷ 1,000 = 293.777) and then compute the CPM:

$$\frac{\$5,208.00}{293.777} = \$17.73$$

7. $67,704 (124 × 42 × 13 = 67,704)

8. Wednesday

9. *Gourmet News* $2,895
   The Gourmet Retailer $3,153

10. a. *Gourmet News:* $14,475 (2,895 × 5 = 14,475)
    b. *The Gourmet Retailer:* $15,765 (3,153 × 5 = 15,765)
    c. Total schedule: $30,240 (14,475 + 15,765 = 30,240)

11. $27,799
    Use the six-time rate for all ads and figure as below:
    Gourmet News: (5 × 2,450) + (1 × 550) = $12,800
    The Gourmet Retailer: (5 × 2,857) + (1 × 714) = $14,999
    Total schedule: $12,800 + $14,999 = $27,799

Market Selections Based on Sales Data

How to Use This Assignment

This assignment can be used for either an in-class or take-home assignment. Because there is a good deal of judgment involved in establishing the criteria to be used in selecting markets, you might want to cover this portion of the assignment in class and have the students do the actual selection as a homework assignment. In any event, it would seem wise to review the assignment in class and discuss each market in terms of its qualifications for inclusion in the list of ten extra-weight markets.

What to Emphasize in Class

Establishing criteria for market selection relies heavily on sound judgment and common sense. Sometimes market selection criteria also must be tempered by knowledge of unusual competitive activity or special sales considerations such as the need to support new account openings.

Some additional points to cover include:

- Definition of BDI (brand development index) and CDI (category development index) and means of developing each.
- Criteria for amount of sales increase from the previous year for each market are usually set at a level that is higher than the average sales increase for all markets.
- The problem posed in this assignment assumes that all of the markets are receiving national advertising. The objective here is to select markets that are to receive *extra* weight.
- You are interested in selecting markets that show potential for growth (high CDI and strong growth in brand sales), as well as those that are well established (high BDI).
- Market selection in this assignment is based on the theory of "fish where the fish are" (i.e., place weight in markets that have already shown sales strength or potential). Because we do not know why sales are low in some markets, we do not have any evidence that additional advertising weight will help improve sales. Point out that low sales could be due to any number of factors unrelated to advertising, such as lack of sales force emphasis or unusual competitive activity.
- The "% change" column in the workbook problem was calculated on the sales figures before they were rounded to the nearest thousand and, therefore, will vary slightly from percentages calculated on the rounded figures.

Answer to Problem for Assignment 9

Suggested criteria for market selection follow. These criteria, except for the percentage change over the previous year, were developed by selecting the median value for each item. These are not absolute figures, and your students might come up with slightly different ones. A suggested range of values is listed for each.

- Annual sales volume of $109,000 or more. (This could be raised to $120,000 or dropped to $100,000.)
- Sales increase of at least 6 percent over previous year. (In no case should this be less than 6 percent—the average for all markets—although it could be raised to 10 percent.)
- Current year BDI of 111 or more. (Range might be 105 to 120.)
- Current BDI level ten points or more above CDI. (Range might be from five to fifteen points.)

Based on the foregoing criteria, the following markets were selected because they met all of the criteria: Chicago, Indianapolis, Los Angeles, Memphis, and Seattle–Tacoma. The following markets were added to the list for the following reasons:

- San Francisco: Was only one point below BDI above CDI.
- Dallas–Ft. Worth: Was only two points below BDI above CDI.
- Philadelphia: Large volume and strong increase, even though BDI was slightly low as was BDI above CDI. BDI was still above 100.
- Detroit: Included for the same reasons as Philadelphia.
- Kansas City: Met all criteria except sales volume.

Because there is some latitude in the establishment of specific criteria, the above list of markets is not absolute. The markets that were not selected follow:

- New York: Volume is high, but market was not included because of low BDI, sales decline, BDI below CDI.
- Boston: Not included because of sales decrease. Might be included because of large sales volume and strong BDI. Reason for sales decrease should be investigated before including.
- Cleveland: Sales increase below par and BDI is below CDI. Might have been included because of large sales volume and strong BDI.
- Washington, D.C.: Low BDI and BDI well below CDI. However, this market could be included because of growth potential as evidenced by sales and BDI increases.
- Pittsburgh: No justification for inclusion.
- St. Louis: Meets only volume criteria; sales decrease and low BDI argue against inclusion.
- Minneapolis–St. Paul: Sales decrease and BDI below CDI. Should determine reason for sales decrease before including on list.
- Baltimore: No justification for inclusion.
- Houston: Large sales decrease and BDI below CDI. Determine reason for sales decrease before considering this market.
- Hartford–New Haven: Shows some strength in terms of BDI, but it was not included because of modest sales increase and low volume.
- Atlanta: No justification for inclusion.
- Buffalo: Shows some potential, but volume and BDI are still low. Worth watching; might be included next year.
- Cincinnati: No justification for inclusion.
- Miami: No justification for inclusion.
- Milwaukee: No justification for inclusion.

Comments

The market selection technique used was simplified for this assignment. In actual practice some weighting would most likely be given to the various criteria. For instance, percentage of sales increase might be given more weight because it shows actual market growth, as contrasted to BDI versus CDI comparisons, which indicate growth potential.

Assuming greater weight for actual sales increases, the market list might be altered to include Detroit and Washington, D.C., and markets such as Boston and Minneapolis–St. Paul might be dropped.

Additional Assignment

Ask students to select (and justify selection of) five more markets they would add if the list were expanded to 15 markets.

Weighting BDI and CDI Data
More Considerations on the Use of Sales Indices

How to Use This Assignment

You can use this assignment to stimulate additional discussion on the use of BDI and CDI numbers. This assignment further explains how you can use these numbers to analyze potential or alternative markets.

You should give students adequate time to work through problems in this assignment prior to in-class discussion. You could ask students to hand in calculations or review calculations in class.

What to Emphasize in Class

Students should review Assignment 9 (Market Selections Based on Sales Data) and any class notes from this earlier discussion. Students should review the specified chapter from *Advertising Media Planning* listed for this assignment (Chapter 8). Reference to CDI and BDI numbers is also made in the solution to the Lux media problem (see Assignment 30).

It is helpful to understand what CDI and BDI numbers represent. These indices (CDI for category sales and BDI for brand sales) reflect the sales rate for a market compared to the average sales rate for all markets (usually on the basis of some form of per-capita sales). Sometimes this index of sales per population segment takes an indirect approach, such as basing BDI on the percentage of total brand sales in a market compared to total retail sales in that market (thus, the population base is adjusted by the per-capita rate of retail spending). However the index is computed, any index above 100 reflects a sales rate higher than that of the average market.

Marketing and media planners find it helpful to review previous sales results so they can estimate what could happen in future sales periods. There are many variables that can help predict market potential and which markets will best respond to media dollars. Sophisticated marketers will use CDI and BDI estimates based on various market factors, but to simplify this assignment, it is assumed that sales in each market will continue to grow at the rate of previous sales growth. Of course, sales estimates are only as good as the assumptions behind such projections or forecasts.

A second consideration discussed in this assignment is whether to emphasize brand or category sales in an analysis of future sales projections and media allocation. Brand sales are frequently viewed as the best indicator of a product's future success. A high BDI probably indicates opportunity for continued success due to certain sales and distribution strengths, or perhaps due to competitive weaknesses in certain markets. CDI becomes an important indicator if increased advertising effort (perhaps for a "new, improved" product) is believed to achieve increases in sales and market share.

The student or beginning media planner might simply choose to ignore emphasis of either BDI or CDI and merely average or total the two indices for each market. This provides equal weight to each index and probably will be a greater error than a considered judgment based on even the most limited information. The conscientious planner should make a determined effort to assign the approximate weight to be placed on BDI or CDI for analysis of markets. Slight shifts in weighting emphasis will have little effect on allocation of media dollars.

Different emphasis of BDI or CDI can be applied to different groups or types of markets. For example, if in certain markets you enjoy excellent distribution but have achieved only moderate awareness of your brand, you would emphasize category sales. If brand volume is low due to poor distribution and lack of trade acceptance, it is unlikely that consumer advertising will be of much help, and you would use current brand sales as the best indicator of which markets will respond to media effort.

A note on calculations: If you ask students to develop future period indices in problem 4 of this assignment, indicate that index numbers will vary slightly according to how numbers are rounded (see calculation notes in solutions section). It might help to assure the conscientious student that slight variations in calculation of indices (e.g., either 126 or 127 for the next future period BDI for market A) will be considered correct and will make virtually no difference in media allocation.

Answers to Problems for Assignment 10

Note that the solution has been calculated by rounding as follows: to nearest whole index number for column 4; to nearest one-hundredth of a percent for column 5; and to nearest tenth of a percent for column 6 for the percentage of budget allocated to the individual market.

Calculations in this assignment will produce a CDI of 187 or 188 and a BDI of 126 or 127 for market A. (The CDI of 188 and BDI of 127 for market A, as stated in the assignment discussion, is the accurate calculation when sales data are not rounded.) However, for this and other markets, an index number within one or two points should be considered a correct calculation.

Solutions and their calculations are as follows:

1. Weighted CDI/BDI index for each of five markets (CDI = 25%; BDI = 75%):

Market	Weighted CDI/BDI
A	139
B	135
C	103
D	69
E	99

Calculations are shown for column 4 of problem 2, which immediately follows.

2.

Market	U.S. TV HHs (%)	Future period indices CDI	Future period indices BDI	Weighted CDI/BDI	Column 1 × Column 4	Five-market media allocation (%)	Five-market media allocation ($)
Column:	(1)	(2)	(3)	(4)	(5)	(6)	(7)
A	1.3%	165	130	139	1.81	14.6	$ 43,800
B	2.7	136	134	135	3.65	29.5	88,500
C	1.8	124	96	103	1.85	15.0	45,000
D	2.3	100	59	69	1.59	12.9	38,700
E	3.5	104	97	99	3.47	28.0	84,000
Five-market total	11.6	120	101	106	12.37	100.0	$300,000
Total U.S.	100.0%	100	100	100	100.00	—	—

Calculation for column 4 (weighted CDI/BDI) is as follows:

Market	+	Weight for CDI × index	=	Weight for BDI × index	Weighted index
A	+	(25% × 165 = 41.3)	+	(75% × 130 = 97.5) =	139
B	+	(25% × 136 = 34.0)	+	(75% × 134 = 100.5) =	135
C	+	(25% × 124 = 31.0)	+	(75% × 96 = 72.0) =	103
D	+	(25% × 100 = 25.0)	+	(75% × 59 = 44.3) =	69
E	+	(25% × 104 = 26.0)	+	(75% × 97 = 72.8) =	99
Totals	+	(25% × 120 = 30.0)	+	(75% × 101 = 75.8) =	106

Calculation for column 5 (Column 1 × Column 4) is as follows:

Market	U.S. TV HHs (%)	×	Weighted CDI/BDI	=	Column 5 (weighted HHs) (%)
A	1.3	×	139	=	1.81
B	2.7	×	135	=	3.65
C	1.8	×	103	=	1.85
D	2.3	×	69	=	1.59
E	3.5	×	99	=	3.47
Five-market total	11.6	×	106	=	12.37*

*Rounding up of index numbers adds up to 12.37.

Calculation for column 6 is as follows (solutions for rounded percentages and to nearest tenth of a percent are shown):

Market	(5)	(6)*	(7)	(6)**	(7)
A	1.81	15%	$ 45,000	14.6%	$ 43,800
B	3.65	30	90,000	29.5	88,500
C	1.85	15	45,000	15.0	45,000
D	1.59	13	39,000	12.9	38,700
E	3.47	28	84,000	28.0	84,000
Totals	12.37	101%	$303,000	100.0%	$300,000

*Percentages rounded.
**Percent to nearest tenth.

3. To allocate media by a "percentage-of-sales" basis, use the BDI chart in Table 10–1 to determine the percentage of sales for each market of the five-market total for a future sales period. Then multiply this percentage for each market by the budget available.

Using question 2 as an example, calculations would be as follows:

Market	Future period sales ($000)	Percent of five-market sales	Media allocation
A	$ 285	14.3	$ 42,900
B	610	30.6	91,800
C	290	14.6	43,800
D	230	11.6	34,800
E	575	28.9	86,700
Totals	$1,990	100.0	$300,000

4. How would each market's media budget allocation be affected if trends continued for an additional future period?

Market	Comment
A	Would hold about even with current allocation
B	Would continue to receive increasing amounts
C	With lowest "plus" sales change, would lose pace
D	Only one of five markets to lose sales, so it would suffer decreases
E	Would enjoy second greatest increase on the basis of prior sales gains

Because the greatest emphasis is being placed against BDI, market B would continue to receive increasingly larger amounts of media, as both brand and category sales are increasing at a faster rate than any other market (brand sales + 20.0% and category sales + 17.0%).

Market E would enjoy the next fastest increase in budget (brand sales + 13.5% and category sales + 11.0%).

Market A would hold about even in its relative importance of the selected five markets, if we assume BDI three times as important as CDI. To the extent we emphasize CDI, this market would increase in relative importance.

Market C, with lowest plus sales gains, would not keep up with average gains of the five-market total and would find its share of media support eroding to the other markets.

Market D would lose share of budget allocation most quickly, as it is the only one of the five markets losing in category and brand sales.

Calculations for projected periods follow (using assumption of CDI = 25%; BDI = 75% as in earlier questions).

Projected CDI for Additional Sales Period

Market	($000)	(%)	Index to TV HHs
A	$ 1,303	2.44	188
B	2,259	4.22	156
C	1,255	2.35	131
D	1,104	2.06	90
E	2,119	3.96	113
Total U.S.	$53,489	100.00	100

Projected BDI for Additional Sales Period

Market	($000)	(%)	Index to TV HHs
A	$ 304	1.64	126*
B	734	3.97	147
C	308	1.67	93
D	225	1.22	53
E	650	3.52	101
Total U.S.	$18,490	100.00	100

*Index is 126 due to rounding. Projections of sales from original sales base without rounding would equal index of 127, as noted in workbook discussion ($285,156 + 6.8% increase = $304,547 for index of 127).

Budget Allocation for Additional Budget Period

Market	Weighted index (CDI = 25%; BDI = 75%)	U.S. TV HHs (%)	Column 1 × Column 2	Media allocation (%)
A	142	1.3	1.85	14.44
B	149	2.7	4.02	31.38
C	103	1.8	1.85	14.44
D	63	2.3	1.45	11.32
E	104	3.5	3.64	28.42
Five-market total	—	11.6	12.81	100

Media Analysis Problems

Understanding Coverage

How to Use This Assignment

This is primarily a take-home assignment in which students may use their textbooks (or other sources of information) as resources to answer the questions.

What to Emphasize in Class

The assignment should help the student clear up the confusion surrounding the term *coverage*. Emphasis in the instructor's lecture should be on the fact that coverage means different things when applied to different media. By writing these differences when answering the questions, students should learn the various meanings of the term.

Answers to Problems for Assignment 11

1. When a network television program has a 98.5 percent coverage, this means that 98.5 percent of all households with at least one television set can tune in to the program, if they want to. They can tune in because they are in the signal area of some station that is carrying the network program. But there is no way of knowing how many actually did tune in. A household television rating would have to provide such information.

   It is conceivable that some network television programs have much less coverage than 98.5 percent. But the coverage is partially the function of the number of stations that carry a program. Some programs are carried by relatively few stations in a network lineup.

2. Solution: 23% (14,500,000 ÷ 63,000,000 = .2301 or 23%)

3. The minimum requirement for you to be counted in a radio coverage measurement is that you own a radio set and that your set is able to pick up the signal of a given radio station.

4. Solution: 61% (128,000 ÷ 210,000 = .609 or 61%). Please note that there is an assumption involved in this statistic, namely that one unit of circulation covers one household.

5. Solution: 66% (422,000 ÷ 640,000 = .659 or 66%)

6. When spot television coverage is 79 percent of the United States, that means that 79 percent of the television households in the country can pick up signals from some station in one (or more) of the 75 markets selected. The coverage figure represents the gross potential audience and the maximum size of a gross audience.

7. 100 percent. Because all the households in each of the 75 markets are required to provide 79 percent coverage of U.S. TV households, the coverage in each of the 75 markets has to be 100 percent.

8. Outdoor coverage represents the number of persons who pass a given out-door showing each day. The outdoor coverage figure represents potential exposure, but it does require that persons at least pass by the medium. Television coverage is also potential, but it does not even require a person's TV set to be turned on.

Use of Cost-per-Thousand (CPM) Concepts

How to Use This Assignment

You should require students to work through the CPM calculations, either as an in-class or take-home assignment. Computations in this assignment are simple, and students can be expected to work the problems in class and then compare their answers with the correct solutions.

What to Emphasize in Class

You should emphasize the following general points:

- It is important to carefully select and define the audience base for CPM calculations.

- CPM comparisons should be for comparable ad units and audiences.

- Remember to divide cost by the audience (a frequent student error is to divide by cost).

- Double-check decimal points (common sense and comparison with other CPM numbers will usually indicate if the decimal point has been misplaced). A frequent problem is failure to multiply cost by 1,000 (or to divide audience by 1,000, whichever is preferred by the student).

- CPM should be carried out to two decimal places, because it reports dollars and cents. A common mistake is to round CPM to one decimal place.

The following are reminders and points that relate directly to problems in this assignment. You might wish to emphasize these before the student is asked to work out the solutions to this assignment.

In problem 1, the audience data are given in thousands, but the cost data provided for magazines A and B in this assignment are stated in actual dollar costs (not rounded).

Note that audience data are usually rounded to the nearest thousand for ease of computation. It is generally best to have students show their work so you can determine whether a different answer is a result of rounding or calculation error. Keep in mind that a difference of a few cents in CPM will make little difference in final selection of media vehicles.

You will probably find it advisable to remind students that the ratings shown in problem 5 are percentages and must be converted to decimals before multiplying to obtain the audience of women.

Answers to Problems for Assignment 12

1. CPM for magazine A: $21,000 ÷ 8,100 = $2.59
   CPM for magazine B: $23,500 ÷ 9,000 = $2.61
   Note that in this problem, audience data are stated in thousands.

2. Magazine B. Magazine B reaches more women aged 18+ and also more women in the important demographic segments (HH3+ and aged 35–49). Magazine B's CPM for women aged 18+ is slightly higher, but its CPM is substantially lower for women in both key demographic segments.

   CPM Comparison for Total Women and Key Demographic Segments

Magazine	Women aged 18+	Women HH3+	Women aged 35–49
A	$2.59	$6.36	$7.00
B	2.61	5.88	5.88

3. Newspaper ad cost: 4 columns × 13 inches × $16 = $832
   CPM circulation: $832 ÷ 125 = $6.66
   Note that the circulation figure was divided by 1,000.

4. Total cost: $832 × .88 = $732.16*
   CPM: $732.16 ÷ 125 = $5.86
   *It is easier to figure the discount rate of 12 percent by multiplying the cost by .88, rather than multiplying by .12 and then subtracting the difference.

5. Program C is the most efficient.

Network program	(1) Audience size (000)	(2) Program cost	CPM (2) ÷ (1)
Program A	13,546 (.14 × 96,760M)	$ 90,000	$6.64
Program B	15,482 (.16 × 96,760M)	97,000	6.27
Program C	18,384 (.19 × 96,760M)	102,000	5.55

Understanding Television Ratings

How to Use This Assignment

Because this assignment deals primarily with the extraction of information from Nielsen data, it makes a good discussion assignment for use in class. The in-class discussion will also provide an opportunity to clear up any misunderstandings and to answer any additional questions students have about television ratings.

What to Emphasize in Class

It would be a good idea to reemphasize that television ratings are estimates of program audience size. They are not exact, nor do they reflect the audience size for a commercial within the program. Other points you might want to make as you review this assignment with the class are the following:

- Review the definitions of terms in this assignment.

- Nielsen national ratings are based on data collected by Audimeters installed in the TV sets of sample homes. Nielsen national audience composition figures are now based on data collected from Peoplemeters installed in sample homes and with which family viewers and visitors can record their viewing. Nielsen is reporting Peoplemeter data in its national reports as well as in local reports in key markets.

- Most local market ratings and audience composition data are based on data from diaries kept by viewers in sample homes. It should be noted that Nielsen is using electronic devices connected to the TV sets of panel homes to collect ratings data in key markets. Further, Nielsen also is installing Peoplemeters in panel homes in key markets to collect audience composition data.

- National ratings are an average for the entire country. Individual market ratings will vary from the national average.

- Nielsen national ratings, in addition to data for the three networks, also include rating and share data for independent and superstations, public broadcasting (PBS), and cable stations (Exhibit 13–1).

- Review the use of share of audience data in media planning (see Sissors and Bumba, 5th ed., Chapter 5).

- Problem 4 of this assignment requires the use of Exhibit 13–3 for the metro area and DMA data and Exhibit 13–1 for the national data.

Answers to Problems for Assignment 13

1.

Program	HHLD Audience	Total Audience
NBC Monday Night Movies	12.3%	20.1%
Love & War	12.7%	14.6%

"Monday Night Movies" is a two-hour show and has a longer time to build total audience compared to the half-hour "Love & War."

2.

Program	HHLD Audience	Share
Nanny	13.8%	21%
Murphy Brown	14.7%	21%

The HUT levels are different. Share of audience is the program's household audience rating as a percentage of households using television (HUT).

3.

Program	Average audience HHs (000)		Women aged 25–54 per 1,000 viewing HHs		Total women aged 25–54
As the World Turns	4,670	×	362	=	1,690,540
General Hospital	5,760	×	439	=	2,528,640
Guiding Light	4,330	×	382	=	1,654,060

4.

Program	Metro areas Rating	Metro areas Share	DMA Rating	DMA Share	National HHLD Aud.	National Share
Nanny	10%	15%	11%	17%	13.8%	21%
Dave's World	17%	26%	16%	25%	13.6%	20%
Fresh Prince of Bel Air	12%	20%	11%	18%	10.6%	16%

National ratings and shares are averages of all local markets and are not necessarily representative of any individual market. In Milwaukee, "The Nanny" generates ratings and shares below the national average, whereas "Dave's World" and "Fresh Prince of Bel Air" garner ratings and shares above the national average.

Additional Assignments

A number of additional assignments can be developed using the source material provided in Exhibits 13–1 through 13–3.

• Have students review the data in Exhibit 13–2 and select the program that would deliver the highest number of women in a particular demographic group (e.g., aged 18–49).

• Using Exhibit 13–1, have students compute the number of households watching cable television or PBS at any given time. The total number of U.S. TV households is shown at the bottom of Exhibit 13–1. If cable TV has a rating of 3.5, then 3,339,000 households would have their sets tuned to a cable station (95,400,000 × .035 = 3,339,000).

- Using Exhibit 13–3, have students compare the ratings and share for network programs versus non-network originated programs.

- Have students, using Exhibit 13–2, compute the audience of women aged 35–49 for selected programs. Because the viewers per 1,000 viewing households (V/1,000) are not given for this demographic group, students will have to develop the number by subtracting the V/1,000 for women aged 18–34 from the number for women aged 18–49. You can also use the same technique to determine V/1,000 for women aged 18–24 (V/1,000 women aged 18–49 minus V/1,000 women aged 25–49).

Estimating Future Television Ratings/Audiences

How to Use This Assignment

This can be used either in class or as a take-home assignment. If students do not normally bring calculators to class, you might want to use it as a take-home project.

What to Emphasize in Class

It is suggested that you review the assignment in class and make sure that students understand the steps for the estimate listed in the assignment of the workbook. It would be a good idea to emphasize that this procedure provides a *rough* estimate of future ratings and audience and that it assumes that the programming in the time period has been consistent.

When you discuss this assignment, point out that ratings should be rounded to the nearest whole number. Many buyers (and planners) follow this procedure because local TV ratings are reported in whole numbers and not in tenths as network ratings are reported.

Answers to Problems for Assignment 14

1.

	Households				Total women				Women aged 18–49			
	Rating	Share	HUT	(000)	Rating	Share	PVT	(000)	Rating	Share	PVT	(000)
Feb.	9	33	28	126	7	31	21	59	6	34	18	27
May	8	33	23	112	5	31	17	42	5	34	14	23

2.

	Households				Total women				Women aged 18–49			
	Rating	Share	HUT	(000)	Rating	Share	PVT	(000)	Rating	Share	PVT	(000)
Nov.	9	38	23	21	6	35	17	12	5	32	15	8
Feb.	11	38	29	26	8	35	22	16	6	32	19	10

3.

	Households				Total women				Women aged 18–49			
	Rating	Share	HUT	(000)	Rating	Share	PVT	(000)	Rating	Share	PVT	(000)
Feb.	8	27	31	57	7	29	24	40	6	28	22	21
May	7	27	25	50	6	29	19	34	4	28	16	14

The calculations necessary to develop the solution to the first problem follow:

1. a. Using the data in Exhibit 14–1, select the proper HUT for Atlanta in May. Note it is 23.

   b. Multiply the May HUT by the estimated share: $23 \times .33 = 7.6$ or 8. This is the estimated household rating for May. Be sure to round the rating to the nearest whole number.
   c. Divide the number of households (in thousands) by the February rating and multiply this answer by the estimated May rating ($126 \div 9 \times 8 = 112$). This is the estimated number of households (in thousands) to be reached in May.

The steps for total women and women aged 18–49 follow:

2. Total Women
   a. From Exhibit 14–1 select the proper May PVT. It is 17.
   b. $17 \times .31 = 5.3$ or 5. This is the May rating for total women.
   c. $59 \div 7 \times 5 = 42.1$ or 42. This is the estimated number of women (in thousands).
3. Women aged 18–49
   a. From Exhibit 14–1 select the proper May PVT. It is 14.
   b. $14 \times .34 = 4.8$ or 5. This is the estimated May rating for women aged 18–49.
   c. $27 \div 6 \times 5 = 22.5$ or 23. This is the estimated number of women aged 18–49 (in thousands).

Additional Assignments

Additional assignments are easy to develop using the data in Exhibit 14–1. Based on the data given for the previous problems, you can have students develop rating and audience estimates for buys in other months. You can make up rating and share data for other markets and have students calculate future ratings and shares.

Broadcast Program Selection

How to Use This Assignment

Because a number of calculations are required, this assignment is probably best used as a take-home assignment. If used in class, students should have calculators to aid in computing audience numbers and CPM.

What to Emphasize in Class

Students will have to use the Nielsen data provided in Exhibit 13–2 to develop the audience figures required for this assignment. You should review the method used in Assignment 13. This is especially important if you have not used Assignment 13. Remember, in selecting audience composition figures from Exhibit 13–2 to be used in computing audience size, the premier to date average (C) figures should be used.

Part (2) of this assignment calls for developing CPM for a package of programs. Although the method is discussed in the assignment, you might want to review this in class.

If Assignment 12 (Use of CPM Concepts) has not been used, you should review the method of calculating CPM.

Answers to Problems for Assignment 15

1. All My Children, One Life to Live, Young and the Restless.
   The data used to calculate the CPM are shown as follows:

Program	Cost	Number of women aged 25–54	CPM
All My Children	$16,500	2,972,750	$5.55*
Another World	8,500	1,117,920	7.60
As the World Turns	12,500	1,690,540	7.39
The Bold and the Beautiful	13,000	1,706,600	7.62
Days of Our Lives	13,800	2,017,710	6.84
General Hospital	16,000	2,528,640	6.33
Guiding Light	11,000	1,654,060	6.65
One Life to Live	14,100	2,299,180	6.13*
Young and the Restless	15,500	2,615,160	5.93*

2. Package 1: All My Children, Another World, Young and the Restless.

CPM calculations for each package follow:

	Program	Cost	Number of women aged 18–49	CPM
Package 1:	All My Children	$16,500	3,277,500	
	Another World	8,500	1,386,440	
	Young and the Restless	15,500	2,812,000	
		$40,500	7,475,940	$5.42
Package 2:	General Hospital	$16,000	2,903,040	
	Guiding Light	11,000	1,792,620	
	One Life to Live	14,100	2,638,560	
		$41,100	7,334,220	$5.60
Package 3:	As the World Turns	$12,500	1,797,950	
	Bold and the Beautiful	13,000	1,764,900	
	Days of Our Lives	13,800	2,499,480	
		$39,300	6,062,330	$6.48

Comments

Because a large part of this assignment deals with the calculations necessary to develop the audience figures and CPM, you should emphasize the need for students to turn in their calculations with this assignment.

Additional assignments can be developed by changing the demographics of the target audience and by changing the program costs.

Estimating Reach and Frequency

How to Use This Assignment

This is essentially a take-home assignment to be handed in for grading. However, it also can be used in the context of a discussion on reach and frequency to show how reach develops.

What to Emphasize in Class

The first and foremost thing to emphasize is that these figures are estimates. They are obtained by studying ratings and reach of many programs and then compiling estimates based on averages.

Then emphasize the way reach develops in various dayparts. For example, in the spot television table, note the differences in reach from daytime to prime time. More reach is possible in prime time because there is a large audience available to see programs. On the other hand, frequency tends to rise very fast at the upper GRP levels in daytime (as reach tends to slow down).

Answers to Problems for Assignment 16

1. a. Ratings for the three programs for one week: $7 + 6 + 5 + 6 = 24$
    b. GRPs for month: $24 \times 4 = 96$
    c. Reach (from Table 16–1) = approximately 42
    d. Frequency: $96 \div 42 = 2.285$ or 2.3

2. a. Estimate household GRPs needed to achieve a 50 percent reach by looking under Day in Table 16–1. Answer: Approximately 160
    b. Look up the conversion factor in the appendix for women aged 18–49 during daytime. Answer: 68
    c. Divide the household GRPs by the conversion factor and multiply the answer by 100. ($160 \div 68 \times 100 = 235$)
    d. Frequency: $235 \div 50 = 4.7$

3. a. Multiply the 300 household GRPs by the conversion factor (from the appendix) for men aged 18–34 for late fringe. ($300 \times .56 = 168$)
    b. Look up in Table 16–2 the reach developed by 224 GRPs in fringe. Answer: Approximately 50 percent
    c. Frequency: $168 \div 50 = 3.36$ or 3.4

4. a. Using Table 16–3, look up the reach generated by 300 GRPs using four networks. Answer: Approximately 44 percent
    b. Frequency: $300 \div 44 = 6.818$ or 6.8

5. a. Using Table 16–4, look up the reach generated by 400 GRPs using five stations. Answer: Approximately 67 percent
    b. Frequency: $400 \div 67 = 5.97$ or 6.0

6. a. Gross circulation coverage: 345,000 ÷ 575,000 = 60 percent
    b. GRPs: 48 × 4 = 192
    c. Reach (from Table 16–5): 65 percent; frequency: 192 ÷ 65 = 2.953 or 3.0

7. a. Determine from Table 16–6 the readers per copy for women aged 25–54:

$$
\begin{aligned}
25\text{--}34 &= .210 \\
35\text{--}44 &= .181 \\
45\text{--}54 &= \underline{.181} \\
&\, .572
\end{aligned}
$$

    b. Target audience reach: 165,000 × .572 = 94,380
    c. Percent reach: 94,380 ÷ 235,000 = 40.16 or 40 percent

Estimating the Reach and Frequency of a Combination of Media Vehicles (Sainsbury Formula)

How to Use This Assignment

This assignment should be a foundation in estimating reach and frequency of vehicles, because it will serve as a means of doing media planning. Although there are other ways of estimating reach and frequency, this is an easy and quick way of doing it. It is very important for other exercises in a media planning course.

Caution: Students might have read or heard that these formulas are inaccurate and therefore should not be used. The formulas do tend to overestimate reach and tend to depress frequency levels. But it should clearly be explained that the purpose of using these formulas is for rough estimates only. For that purpose, they are excellent. However, with a correction factor built in to the formulas, they tend to be accurate enough for learning media planning. When students work in the media planning departments of advertising agencies, they will have the opportunity of using computers to calculate more accurate formulas. The penalty for using more accurate formulas is the necessity of taking much more time than is worthy for learning the basics of media planning. Even account executives or marketing practitioners with little or no media training will use these formulas at times simply because they are quick and easy to use and give an approximation that can later be improved with computer-programmed formulas.

What to Emphasize in Class

Students should learn both formulas and use the more expedient one for a given situation. The original formula lends itself to use with a calculator. But because it requires entering a great deal of information, there is a greater margin of error, especially when four or more vehicles are being analyzed.

The other formula is a step-wise technique, which means that the student first calculates the reach of a pair of vehicles and then adds another vehicle, and another, etc. It is easier to trace errors in the second formula when four or more vehicles are being analyzed.

Students must recognize that the duplication number is an estimate based on probability. This makes estimating quicker and easier, but it results in less accurate data. The estimate of duplication is easiest to see in the second formula, where the reach of one vehicle is multiplied by the reach of the second vehicle (in percentage form). Note that this estimate works in percentages, but not in raw numbers. However, the percentages can always be transformed to numbers by multiplying the percentage by an audience base. For example, if we want to estimate the reach of one TV program and another, we might find the reach of one is 20 percent and the reach of the other is 40 percent. By multiplication, the duplication percent is .0800 or 8 percent. If the audience base of reach is 50,029,000 women in the U.S. aged 18–49, then 8 percent times 50,029,000 will provide a number of those duplicated by both programs (or 4,002,000).

Urge students to find the reach of a vehicle in terms of target audience, not circulation or total audiences in general. Simmons data provide the reach of magazines, and Assignment 18 explains how to estimate the target reach of television programs.

It should be obvious by now that this formula can be used to find the combined net reach of any kind of vehicle if the data for each individual reach are known. Therefore it is possible to combine the reach of network TV with spot TV, with radio, with newspapers, etc. That is another reason for using the formula.

Remind students that they should reduce reach figures when they are combining three or more vehicles. This will help reduce the problem of excessive reach that the formula tends to generate. The answers shown have been modified whenever three or more vehicles are involved.

Finally, urge students to transform percentages into decimals when multiplying them in order to help locate the decimal point. For example, 36.8% = .368. Percentages can be *added* in their percent form, but they usually are easier to *multiply* in decimal form.

Answers to Problems for Assignment 17

The original formula was used to calculate the answers to the problems in this assignment. The other formula would work just as well, however.

1.

	January Reach	January Frequency	February Reach	February Frequency	March Reach	March Frequency
National reach/frequency	59	2.1	67	2.2	70	2.4
Spot market R/F	59	2.1*	81**	3.6	83**	3.5

*During January the reach and frequency are the same in the spot markets as they are nationally, because no spot market media has been scheduled.
**These reach figures have been reduced by 5 percent because three different vehicles are being used.

Spot market reach and frequency for February were calculated as follows:

Reach:

Net TV	$100 - 52 = 48$
National magazines	$100 - 32 = 68$
Spot TV	$100 - 55 = 45$

$.48 \times .68 \times .45 = .147$ or 15 percent nonreach
$100 - 15 \times .95 = .808$ or 81 percent net reach

Frequency:

Net TV	$52 \times 2.0 =$	104.0 GRPs
National magazines	$32 \times 1.3 =$	41.6 GRPs
Spot TV	$55 \times 2.7 =$	<u>148.5</u> GRPs
		294.1 GRPs

$\dfrac{294}{81} = 3.63$ or 3.6 frequency

2. Combination ABC: Reach 74%, Frequency 3.6
   Combination ABD: Reach 73%, Frequency 3.6
   Combination ACD: Reach 65%, Frequency 3.9
   Combination BCD: Reach 67%, Frequency 3.8

   (All of the reach figures have been reduced by 5 percent because three different vehicles are being used.) The combination that best fulfills the objective of maximum reach and a minimum frequency of at least 3.5 is ABC. The combination generating the highest frequency level is ACD.

Converting Television Household Data to Target Audience Reach and Frequency

How to Use This Assignment

It can be used in class or as a homework assignment, whichever fits your needs best.

What to Emphasize in Class

Call students' attention to the necessity of knowing the four-week reach and frequency of target audiences. Although it is relatively easy to find these data for households, that kind of information is not adequate, because media planning is based on reaching precise target audiences, not just households.

Tell students to round the turnover number to the nearest one-tenth and to use the rounded figure in their calculations of reach. Also point out to students the key at the bottom of Exhibit 18–1 so they know that ratings for specific demographic segments are reported on line A.

Answers to Problems for Assignment 18

1. "CBS Sunday Movie"

Household turnover:	$42.8 \div 18.6 = 2.3$
Women aged 25–54 reach:	$13.5 \times 2.3 = 31.1$
Women aged 25–54 frequency:	$(13.5 \times 4) \div 31.1 = 1.7$

2. "Beverly Hills, 90210"

Household turnover:	$22.6 \div 11.2 = 2.0$
Working women reach:	$9.1 \times 2.0 = 18.2$
Working women frequency:	$(9.1 \times 4) \div 18.2 = 2.0$

3. "Coach"

Household turnover:	$18.6 \div 9.8 = 1.9$
Men aged 55+ reach:	$8.2 \times 1.9 = 15.6$
Men aged 55+ frequency:	$(8.2 \times 4) \div 15.6 = 2.1$

4. "Blossom"

Household turnover:	$22.4 \div 10.2 = 2.2$
Total teens reach:	$11.3 \times 2.2 = 24.9$
Total teens frequency:	$(11.3 \times 4) \div 24.9 = 1.8$

   "Beverly Hills, 90210"

Household turnover:	$22.6 \div 11.2 = 2.0$
Total teens reach:	$11.8 \times 2.0 = 23.6$
Total teens frequency:	$(11.8 \times 4) \div 23.6 = 2.0$

5. Conversion factor,
   daytime, spot TV, women
      aged 25–54:   .64*

   Household GRPs: 500

   Target rating points, women
      aged 25–54: $500 \times .64 = 320$

   Women aged 25–54, reach: 56**

   Women aged 25–54, frequency: $320 \div 56 = 5.7$

*From appendix, Table 1.
**From Table 16–2, Assignment 16.

Note: Using conversion factors to calculate target reach is different from using household audience turnover factors. Which is most accurate? Turnover factors tend to be more accurate because they are based on measured data that are more current.

Estimating Reach and Frequency for Radio

How to Use This Assignment

This assignment can be used either in class or as a take-home assignment. If used as a take-home assignment, we suggest you consider adding some extra calculations, which are discussed under "Additional Assignments."

What to Emphasize in Class

It would be a good idea to review this assignment in class to make sure that students understand the definitions of Arbitron terms and how the data are reported in Exhibit 19–2. Be sure to remind students that they must add two zeros to the AQH and cume persons figures, because they are reported in hundreds (00).

Some students will wonder why they cannot use the cume and AQH ratings as reported by Arbitron instead of having to calculate them using persons data. They could use the ratings as reported *if* they were dealing with only one age group. However, when age groups must be combined, the only accurate way to do it is to add the AQH or cume persons and then compute the percentage based on the total number of persons in the combined age groups. Otherwise, it would be necessary to develop a weighting factor for each individual age group.

You also might want to remind students as they develop the AQH and cume ratings that these are percentages and they should be familiar with how they relate to their decimal equivalents. Also remind students that reach figures should be rounded to the nearest whole percent and frequency figures to the nearest tenth.

Finally, point out that column J on the worksheet calls for the number of spots in *four* weeks, not the number of spots per week as given in the background for this assignment.

Answers to Problems for Assignment 19

1. Reach: 70%, frequency: 5.8 (409 ÷ 70 = 5.8)
2. Reach: 70%, frequency: 7.3 (510 ÷ 70 = 7.3)
3. Reach: 79%, frequency: 6.2 (486 ÷ 79 = 6.2)

The completed sample worksheet detailing the calculations needed to arrive at the answers follows:

Worksheet: Radio Four-Week Reach and Frequency

Target Group W 25-44
Population 82200

Reach _____
Frequency _____

A Stations	B Cumes	C Population	D Cume Ratings (B÷C)	E Total Cume Ratings	F Duplication & Lack of Potential Factor	R Reach (E x F)	G Avg. Qtr. Hr.	H Population	I Qtr. Hr. Ratings (G÷H)	J # of Spots Over 4 Weeks	K GRP (I x J)	L Total GRPs (80 Spts.)	
KKRD	25600		31				1400		1.7	48	82	(102)	
KEYN	18700		23				1400		1.7	48	82	(102)	
KRBB	20200		25				1800		2.2	48	106	(132)	
KZSN-FM	24800		30	Add ratings for stations needed & give total.			2400		2.9	48	139	(174)	
		82200 Population		109 Total	.64	= 70		82200 Population				Add GRPs for stations needed & give total. 409 Total	5.8
					2 stations use .72 / 3 stations use .68 / 4 stations use .64 / 5 or more use .62							(510)	7.3
KXLK	15500		19		128	.62	79			1.6	48	77	486
													6.2

Additional Assignments

The exhibits provided with this assignment offer a variety of additional assignment opportunities. Variations can be developed merely by changing the demographic profile of the target audience, the stations to be used, or the number of commercials per week.

Another variation is to establish a reach or frequency goal and let the students select the stations and number of spots per week needed to reach that goal.

The following list of population figures by age/sex for Wichita enables you to develop additional assignments using different demographics.

Men	18–24:	22,900	Women	18–24:	22,700
	25–34:	43,500		25–34:	42,200
	35–44:	41,000		35–44:	40,000
	45–49:	14,900		45–49:	15,400
	50–54:	11,500		50–54:	12,500
	55–64:	19,800		55–64:	21,000
	65 +:	24,200		65 +:	36,100
	18 +:	177,800		18 +:	189,900

Teens 12–17:   42,800
Total Persons 12 +:   410,500

How to Estimate Reach and Frequency from Competitive Media Expenditure Data

How to Use This Assignment

You might want to use this as a take-home assignment or as an in-class exercise, depending on whether students clearly understand how to proceed. If they are not clear, then use this in class. Afterward, assign another problem: to calculate reach and frequency from the Lux assignment for one competitor, from the data in the example of this assignment.

What to Emphasize in Class

Competitive media expenditure data are available from syndicated services such as LNA or BAR. If those are available to you, then the method of estimating reach and frequency represents no problem. But often the only thing that is available is a total dollar figure expended by a competitor. In such a case, emphasize the need for further estimating the allocations to media. It will be quite difficult to make these estimations if a competitor used a large number of media. But it will be easy if they used only one or two. However, students will still have to estimate the probable percentage allocated to the two media.

Emphasize the fact that although these reach and frequency estimates are very rough, they are much better than sheer guesswork.

Furthermore, there will be times when you know precisely how your brand spends its money, but you will have to use syndicated data to estimate competitors' usages. In such a case, use data for your brand taken from competitive syndicated sources even though you have more accurate data for your brand available. Through this practice, you thereby place all estimation data in the same (or similar) frame of reference.

Be sure to point out that there are usually fewer people in a given demographic segment watching or exposed to a medium than there are households exposed to it. Therefore, it is necessary to convert household gross rating points to target gross rating points. However, like many pieces of media data, these conversions are only estimates. They might even differ from agency to agency, although the differences are not large.

Answer to Problem for Assignment 20

1. Multiply the yearly budget by 15 percent to learn how much was spent in August.

    $8,500,000 × .15 = $1,275,000 budget for August (estimated)

2. Determine how much of the $1,275,000 was spent in each daypart, as follows:

$$\begin{array}{lll}
\text{Prime time:} & \$1,275,000 \times .50 = & \$637,500 \\
\text{Day:} & 1,275,000 \times .25 = & 318,750 \\
\text{Fringe:} & 1,275,000 \times .25 = & 318,750
\end{array}$$

Here are the calculations for the problem above:

	1 Cost per rating point[a]	2 House-hold GRPs	3 Conversion factor[b]	4 TRPs (Target GRPs)	5 Estimated reach	6 Estimated frequency
Prime-time Network	$14,000	46	.65	30	18	1.7

Column 2. 637,500 ÷ 14,000 = 46

Column 4. Multiply HH GRPs by conversion factor from appendix Table 2

Column 5. Look up reach table in Assignment 16. Because there is no reach for a GRP level of 30, use a ratio from table: $100 : 61 = 30 : x.\ x = 18$

Column 6. Divide TRPs by reach

Daytime Network	$3,168	101	.68	69	30	2.3

Column 2. 318,750 ÷ 3,168 = 101

Column 4. Multiply HH GRPs by conversion factor from appendix Table 2

Column 5. Look up reach table in Assignment 16. Because there is no reach for a GRP level of 69, use a ratio from table: $100 : 43 = 69 : x.\ x = 30$

Column 6. Divide TRPs by reach

Late Fringe Network	$7,177	44	.62	27	11	2.5

Column 2. 318,750 ÷ 7,177 = 44

Column 4. Multiply HH GRPs by conversion factor from appendix Table 2

Column 5. Look up reach table in Assignment 16. Because there is no reach for a GRP level of 27, use a ratio from table: $100 : 42 = 27 : x.\ x = 11$

Column 6. Divide TRPs by reach

Sainsbury (Assignment 17) for net reach

Prime time	18	
Daytime	30	Net reach = 47[c]
Late fringe	11	

Frequency (TRPs ÷ Reach)

Prime time TRPs	30	
Daytime TRPs	69	126 ÷ 47 = 2.7
Late fringe TRPs	27	
Total	126	

[a]From appendix Table 3.
[b]From appendix Table 2.
[c]Reduced by 5 percent, because three vehicles were being combined.

Note that there is some danger in transforming reach into a ratio problem because the answer sometimes makes no sense. Reach is not directly proportional to GRPs; the reach curve changes shape radically as GRPs rise. Reach calculated that way might be much too high or low. Then common sense must take over and an estimate must be made. At other times a ratio formula seems to provide a reasonable reach. The decision about the best reach has to be made on what is called "face validity," meaning that it must "look reasonable."

$$\text{Reach} = \frac{\text{view}}{\text{pop}}$$

Determining the Effective Frequency and Reach of a Media Plan

How to Use This Assignment

This assignment involves a relatively new media planning concept: effective reach and frequency. The student should read material in Chapters 6 and 9 of Sissors and Bumba as a basis, but they should also read other materials as available. The most important value of this assignment is its speculative nature. Students should concentrate not only on media practices of the present, but the future as well. It is likely that effective frequency, at least, will become a major practice in media planning sometime in the future.

Nevertheless, students should be urged to ask, "How can media planners go beyond the present usage of reach and frequency?" The effective frequency concept is one of the ways. It has generated much discussion among expert media planners. Students should see its value by studying the requirements of this assignment.

What to Emphasize in Class

Encourage students to first know what reach and frequency data mean to strategic planning. They tell the planner how many prospects will have an opportunity to see ads and also provide an average number of potential exposures. But reach and frequency tell the planner nothing about the effectiveness of the media plan. Will the plan result in sales?

The answer to the last question is that media plays a role in selling, namely, getting ads to the prospects. But when that time comes, the creative effort of ads takes over. Therefore, the best that media can do is to be sure to reach enough prospects enough times per month or year.

If we want to add another dimension to reach and frequency, we might ask, "How does media, in conjunction with creative effort, work to sell?" Experts believe that when an ad is seen enough times, it has better selling potential than if it is seen once. The question is, how many times is optimum? That is where effective frequency becomes significant. Effective frequency suggests that one or two exposures is not enough, but three or more might be enough. There is great disagreement here about whether 2–3 exposures are optimal. Or are 3–10 exposures optimal? Therefore, remind students that planners do not know the answer, but they have clues through various kinds of research.

Probably the most controversial part of the concept is in the decision to accept media vehicle exposures as equivalent to advertising exposures. Almost all of the research on this subject has been done by studying exposures to advertising. But most often, a media plan with a vehicle frequency of three does not deliver an advertising frequency of three. Why? Because it is possible for consumers to see a vehicle like *Reader's Digest* and yet miss many of the ads in the vehicle. So this controversy should be emphasized. There is no solution to the controversy at present. But it should be clear that one media vehicle exposure does not equal one advertising exposure.

Also emphasize that when one is talking about effective frequency, effective reach is always assumed to be part of the concept. For every level of frequency there is corresponding reach.

Answer to Problem for Assignment 21

Shown later are estimations of how much to add to or subtract from 3+ frequency. Remind students that there are no absolutes, and even the numbers that come from this assignment tend to be subjective. But the value of this assignment is to make students think about the fact that 3+ frequency must be an oversimplification for setting effective frequency levels. Those who believe in Joseph Ostrow's advice to the media planning world are forced to start using more definitive criteria for setting optimum frequency levels.

Marketing Factors That Affect Effective Frequency

Established brands	−.2	−.1	+.1	(+.2)	New brands
High market share	−.2	−.1	+.1	(+.2)	Low market share
Dominant brand in market	−.2	−.1	+.1	(+.2)	Smaller, less well-known brands
High brand loyalty	−.2	−.1	+.1	(+.2)	Low brand loyalty
Long purchase cycle	(−.2)	−.1	+.1	+.2	Short purchase cycle (high volume segments)
Product used occasionally	−.2	−.1	+.1	(+.2)	Product used daily
			+.1	(+.2)	Needed to beat competition
			+.1	(+.2)	Advertising to older consumers, or children

Copy Factors That Affect Effective Frequency

Simple copy	−.2	−.1	+.1	(+.2)	Complex copy
Copy more unusual than competition	−.2	−.1	+.1	(+.2)	Copy less unusual than competition
Continuing campaign	−.2	−.1	+.1	(+.2)	New copy campaign
Product sell copy	−.2	−.1	+.1	(+.2)	Image type copy
Single kind of message	−.2	−.1	+.1	(+.2)	More different kinds of messages
To avoid wearout: New messages	(−.2)	−.1	+.1	+.2	Older messages
Larger ad units	(−.2)	−.1	+.1	+.2	Small ad units

Media Factors That Affect Effective Frequency

Lower ad clutter	(−.2)	−.1	+.1	+.2	High ad clutter
Compatible editorial environment	(−.2)	−.1	+.1	+.2	Incompatible environment
Attentiveness high	(−.2)	−.1	+.1	+.2	Attentiveness low
Continuous advertising	−.2	(−.1)	+.1	+.2	Pulsed or flighted advertising
Few media used	−.2	(−.1)	+.1	+.2	Many media used
Opportunities for media repetition	−.2	(−.1)	+.1	+.2	Fewer opportunities

Source: Joseph W. Ostrow, "Setting Frequency Levels," in *Effective Frequency: The State of the Art.* Copyright 1982. Reprinted by permission.

From the circled criteria, we find that the pluses add to 2.3 and the minuses add to 1.6. However, there are at least two more criteria that could have been added to make the frequency level more meaningful:

Low-involvement product	+.2
Competitors highly entrenched	+.2
Sum of extra criteria	+.4

Final Tabulations

1. Add the two extra criteria to the +2.3 developed previously:

	+ .4
	+2.3
Total of pluses	+2.7

2. Subtract the minuses:

	−1.6
Total	+1.1

3. Add +1.1 to +3.0 as follows:

Old effective frequency score	+3.0
Final tally of pluses and minuses	+1.1
Effective frequency recommended	+4.1

Use of Gross Impressions in Media Planning

How to Use This Assignment

Although you could use this as a take-home assignment, we recommend that you use it as part of a lecture-demonstration presentation. The concept is relatively easy to understand. Therefore, if you were lecturing on the subject, you could conclude with an in-class problem.

What to Emphasize in Class

There are two important things to emphasize in class: (a) what the value is of knowing the gross impressions of a media plan; and (b) how gross impressions relate to the net reach of a plan.

The value of knowing gross impressions should be clear: The calculation of gross impressions gives the planner a single number by which he or she can compare one group of media alternatives with another. These numbers are evidence that one set of media is better than another (other things being equal).

There are a number of aspects to the relationship of gross impressions and net reach. The media plan with the largest number of gross impressions sometimes also has the largest reach, but net reach is usually affected by something other than gross impressions. It is affected by the ability of media recommended in a plan to deliver a large number of different target audience members. So it is the diversity of media used in the plan—not gross impressions, necessarily—that determines how much net reach will develop.

However, advise the students not to spend undue time speculating about the relationship between gross impressions and net reach. That relationship is not the main reason that gross impressions are used in media planning. The most important reason is that formulas for calculating net reach are not as accurate as we would like them to be. Therefore, the media planner needs more evidence for making the correct decision from among a number of alternatives. Net reach calculations comprise one piece of evidence. But gross impressions are an additional piece of evidence that simply supports net reach. Obviously, other evidence is also needed, such as cost per thousand, frequency levels, and patterns of continuity.

Answer to Problem for Assignment 22

Students should solve this problem in two steps. First, they should calculate the number of gross impressions for each plan. Next, they should calculate the cost per thousand for gross impressions for each plan. The plan with the lowest cost per thousand is the best buy (other things being equal). Following are the calculations:

Step 1

Media selected	Targets reached		Number of insertions		Gross impressions for each medium
Media Plan A					
Magazine A	9,200,000	×	4	=	36,800,000
Net TV B	2,150,000	×	8	=	17,200,000
Spot TV	1,875,000	×	18	=	33,750,000
				Total	87,750,000
Media Plan B					
Magazine D	8,900,000	×	3	=	26,700,000
Net TV E	2,850,000	×	10	=	28,500,000
Net TV F	8,500,000	×	4	=	34,000,000
				Total	89,200,000

Step 2

Media selected	Cost per single ad/ commercial		Number of insertions		Total cost
Cost of Plan A					
Magazine A	$94,000	×	4	=	$376,000
Net TV B	20,500	×	8	=	164,000
Spot TV	4,600	×	18	=	82,800
				Total	$622,800
Cost of Plan B					
Magazine D	$82,000	×	3	=	$246,000
Net TV E	9,000	×	10	=	90,000
Net TV F	90,000	×	4	=	360,000
				Total	$696,000

Cost per thousand for plan A
  $622,800 × 1,000 ÷ 87,750,000 = $7.10 CPM gross impressions

Cost per thousand for plan B
  $696,000 × 1,000 ÷ 89,200,000 = $7.80 CPM gross impressions

Media plan A is the best buy. There is relatively little difference in total gross impressions (less than 2 percent), but plan A has a substantially (almost 10 percent) lower CPM.

Media Strategy Planning Problems

Strategic Impressions in Media Planning

How to Use This Assignment

This is a take-home assignment primarily. It can be used separately or as part of an explanation of how to produce a media plan. The ideas are relatively simple.

What to Emphasize in Class

The most important idea to emphasize is that a target market for a media plan may be multisegmented. The term *target market* implies that a single demographic group is to be reached. But often there are a number of groups that comprise a target.

Second, it is important to caution students about weighting these various groups. The importance of each group, usually, is a function of its degree of product usage, as measured by the syndicated services. However, some portion of the weighting decision is required when the planner decides to concentrate on heavy users alone, or heavy users in combination with moderate users. Finally, a media planner with considerable experience will want to weight the various groups arbitrarily based on experience. Students obviously do not have such experience.

Another consideration that should be emphasized is that the weighting of strategic impressions works best when a single demographic class is used, such as age or sex. This does not mean that two or more different classes could not be used, but that a single class is easier to work with in deciding weights.

Finally, the weighting of impressions is only a preliminary step in a media plan. When the plan has been completed, it is the responsibility of the planner to be able to prove that the media selections will deliver impressions in the manner that is consistent with the chosen weights. Without this final requirement, there is no point in determining strategic impressions.

Answer to Problem for Assignment 23

In order to complete the assignment, students will combine age categories for both heavy and moderate users, as well as for combinations of age groups. (There are five age segments, but these will be reduced to three.)

1, 2. Calculate new index numbers:

Ages	U.S. population		Number of users
18–34	27,135	18–34 heavy users	5,038
		18–34 medium users	6,441
		Total 18–34	11,479
35–44	16,640	35–44 heavy users	3,719
		35–44 medium users	4,511
45–54	11,752	45–54 heavy users	2,523
		45–54 medium users	2,718
Total	28,392	Total 35–54	13,471
55–64	11,215	55–64 heavy users	2,024
		55–64 medium users	1,910
65+	14,770	65+ heavy users	1,893
		65+ medium users	3,294
Total	25,985	Total 55+	9,121

a. Total heavy users   15,197
    Total medium users   18,874
                      34,071

b. % of female homemakers' (FHM) population (34,071 ÷ 81,512 = 1.8%)

c. % of all 18–34 FHM population   (11,479 ÷ 27,135 = 42.3%)
    % of all 35–54 FHM population   (13,471 ÷ 28,392 = 47.4%)
    % of all 55+ FHM population   (9,121 ÷ 25,985 = 35.1%)

d. Calculate new index numbers as follows:
    18–34   (42.3 ÷ 41.8 =   101 index)
    35–54   (47.4 ÷ 41.8 = 113 index)
    55+   (35.1 ÷ 41.8 =   84 index)

e. Allocation of strategic impressions:

	Index	Impression percentages
18–34	101	34%
35–54	113	38
55+	84	28
Total strategic impressions		100%

3. The data show how the decisions were made. If, however, the student had other data showing that one of the age groups was more important for our brand, the student might add some extra weight, arbitrarily, to that group.

4. The student would have used the All Users category if the purchasers of the brand were spread fairly evenly among all user classes. Or the student might not be sure of which groups buy this brand. In that case, the student would use All Users. Finally, if the student were trying to expand the market, the target groups would be expanded.

Quintile and Frequency Distributions in Media Planning

How to Use This Assignment

This assignment requires a clear understanding of quintile distributions and a thoughtful study of the exhibits. It can be used for in-class discussion or as a take-home assignment.

This assignment is provided to help the student use quintile distributions, data that are used quite often in media planning and marketing analysis. Students can see these data for themselves in SMRB and MRI books used by all major advertising agencies and many schools for media planning purposes.

It is not necessary to calculate quintile distributions, just as it is not necessary to calculate frequency distributions. But students should know how to interpret these distributions. This assignment is intended to strengthen the students' understanding of the theoretical foundations of media planning and provide information for planners to use to defend their media selections.

What to Emphasize in Class

There are three main ideas that should be emphasized. First, a quintile distribution can be better than a frequency distribution, because it offers a quicker way to get at the meaning of the numbers. Second, index numbers are better than simple percentages such as those used in column B of Simmons, because index numbers compare percentage of usage against population distribution. Therefore, index numbers are better indicators of sales potential. However, be alert to high index numbers that are derived from small population or user bases. Finally, warn students that small differences in index numbers such as the difference between a 108 and a 112 are not valid. Urge them to watch for differences of over ten index points.

Answers to Problems for Assignment 24

1. Newspapers, magazines, and television all have above-average index numbers for quintiles I and II. Newspapers have a combined index of 219 for quintiles I and II, magazines a combined index of 207, and television a combined index of 217 for prime time and 213 for total television viewing. Likewise, these media also have below-average index numbers for quintiles IV and V.

2. Outdoor, with a combined index of 187 (13 points below average) for quintiles I and II, would be the least likely medium to select to reach users of caffeinated instant and freeze-dried coffee.

3. When only heavy users are considered, newspapers, with a combined index of 233, and television, with indices of 217 for prime time and 229 for total TV viewing, are good choices. However, magazines, although appropriate to

reach all users, have a combined index of just 195 against heavy users and in general would not seem a viable choice, although special interest magazines, e.g., women's service, might be appropriate.

4. Consumers use the Yellow Pages primarily to find the location of merchants who carry a particular type of merchandise or a specific brand of product that is not regularly purchased. Consumers (especially female homemakers) know where to purchase instant and freeze-dried coffee and would have no need to refer to the Yellow Pages. Use of the Yellow Pages would not serve a useful purpose for a coffee brand.

5. The reason each quintile does not have precisely 20 percent is that the criteria for each quintile, for each medium, are very different. Therefore, the distribution of audience members among the five quintiles does not break nicely at 20 percent. As an example, note how few newspaper readers there are in quintile I. The criteria for selection required that women read five or more different newspapers, and there were fewer than 20 percent who met that requirement. However, if the criteria were changed to four or more, it would result in too many respondents being placed in quintile I and a percentage well over 20 percent. The requirements for each quintile and for each medium have been adjusted to make the breaks come as close to 20 percent as possible.

Proving That a Media Plan Delivers the Planned Objectives

How to Use This Assignment

This assignment should be used after students have mastered all major parts of media planning concepts and techniques. It is an advanced assignment that helps planners prove that their decisions do what they were supposed to do.

Because some courses of study are relatively short (those on the quarter rather than semester system), there might be time only to discuss the technique of doing the assignment. But it is preferable to cover in detail both the concept and the technique.

Actually, this is really just an exercise in using gross impressions to prove that objectives were met. (Gross impressions have been discussed earlier in this workbook.)

What to Emphasize in Class

The student should be introduced to the problem that this assignment addresses: How do I know that I made the correct media selections? The answer and solution are to be found in proving that gross impressions matched objectives.

In doing the calculations, it is important to note that ten ads were purchased in each of *Better Homes & Gardens* (*BH&G*) and *Reader's Digest,* but 12 commercials were purchased on "60 Minutes." That means that in finding the gross impressions, the audiences delivered by each magazine must be multiplied by ten, but the audiences delivered by "60 Minutes" must be multiplied by 12.

Students should also be aware where the data come from that are used in this assignment. Simmons and MRI report magazine data, and Nielsen reports cross-tabulated television viewing data.

Finally, have students review Assignment 22 if they are in doubt about how to calculate gross impressions.

Answer to Problem for Assignment 25

Gross Impression Analysis

Demographic segments	BH&G (000)	Reader's Digest (000)	"60 Minutes" (000)	Total	Percentage	Goal	Index
Age							
18–34	112,070	142,430	63,120	317,620	26.7%	25.0%	107
35–54	122,260	164,250	113,520	400,030	33.7	35.0	96
55+	98,370	181,960	190,920	471,250	39.6	40.0	99
				1,188,900	100.0%	100.0%	
Income							
Under $20,000	86,810	142,480	90,636	319,926	26.9%	25.0%	108
$20,000–$40,000	114,130	169,990	110,520	394,640	33.2	35.0	95
$40,000+	131,750	176,170	166,404	474,324	39.9	40.0	100
				1,188,890	100.0%	100.0%	
County size							
A	112,210	165,370	144,360	421,940	35.5%	37.0%	96
B	108,850	164,020	115,440	388,310	32.7	33.0	99
C and D	111,630	159,250	107,760	378,640	31.8	30.0	106
				1,188,890	100.0%	100.0%	

Analysis of this data, especially the index numbers, shows that the objectives have been met rather well. One must remember that a difference of less than ten index points is not a significant difference.

Reach and Frequency Analysis

	Adults aged 55+ delivered (000)	Reach percent[a]	Net reach monthly
Reach of *BH&G*	9,837	19.4%	
Reach of *Reader's Digest*	18,196	35.8	61.3[b]
Reach of "60 Minutes"	15,910	31.3	

[a]Base of adults 55+ (50,764,000 used).
[b]Net reach calculated using Sainsbury formula and reduced by 5% as three vehicles were used.

The net reach goal was 70 percent of adults 55+, and this plan delivered 64.5 percent. More reach would be desirable, but this plan is not too far off target in this area. The frequency of the three vehicles is 1.3, but the goal was 3, so the plan is inadequate in terms of frequency. Perhaps the frequency goal was too optimistic considering the vehicles being used. The frequency was calculated for a four-week period as follows:

Reach of *BH&G*	= 19.4
Reach of *Reader's Digest*	= 35.8
Reach of "60 Minutes"	= 31.3
GRP	86.5 (86.5 ÷ 61.3 = 1.4 frequency)

Writing Media Objectives

How to Use This Assignment

This assignment requires adequate time for students to study the marketing background before proceeding to write the media objectives. Therefore, you will want to have students read over the assignment before covering it in class, or you can use it as a take-home assignment.

What to Emphasize in Class

Stress the fact that media objectives deal with *what* the media plan is to accomplish and should not deal with *how* it is to be accomplished. Properly written objectives should not spell out specific media choices such as magazines, network television, etc. Go over the marketing situation review in class to make sure that the students understand the material presented there. You might want to explain some of the terms used in that section:

- **ACV distribution.** All commodity volume distribution—the percentage of sales of all commodities accounted for by the stores carrying this brand. In this example, the brand has distribution in stores in New England that account for 66 percent of the food store volume done in New England. Nielsen reports distribution in this manner, which is more valuable than a simple store-count distribution figure that does not take into account the sales volume done by each store.

- **Nielsen bimonthly reporting periods.** DJ = December/January, FM = February/March, etc.

- **"Working media" budget.** Refers to the fact that the entire budget is to be used for actual media purchases and that it does not contain funds that are to be used for production expenses or nonmedia promotion costs such as coupon redemption or sweepstakes prizes.

Answer to Problem for Assignment 26

Suggested objectives are detailed here. Although students will not write in the same style, they should cover the basic point of each objective. See explanatory notes following each objective.

Target Audience
Primary audience—advertising should be directed toward the primary purchaser, female homemakers aged 25–54 in middle- and upper-income groups, with children and living in urban areas.

Note: Age and the presence of children are not specified in the marketing background, but they are strongly suggested by the family size of three or more.

Additional Audience

Direct advertising toward the food store trade, particularly food store managers and chain headquarters.

Note: This additional audience objective is important as it helps meet a specific marketing objective (4). Students should recognize the food store trade as an important audience.

Geographic Coverage

Provide national coverage to support national sales and distribution, emphasizing, to the extent possible, urban areas of 200,000 population and above.

Provide advertising heavy-up in regions of above-average sales as evidenced by high brand development indices. These include the Pacific and especially the East Central region, where increased competitive activity is expected.

Note: This objective should cover both the need for national coverage and the need for regional heavy-up per marketing objectives 1 and 2. The West Central region might also be included (BDI 102) with the proviso that it be included if funds are available. Although high CDIs in the New England and Mid-Atlantic regions indicate potential, below-average distribution and BDIs would suggest waiting to include those areas until distribution is increased.

Continuity (or Pattern of Scheduling)

Year-long continuity is desirable, but it is especially important to provide seasonal heavy-up during the peak sales period, November through April.

Note: This objective assumes that the 109 ON index indicates heavier sales in November leading into the peak season, and the 103 AM index indicates declining sales in May leading out of the peak season. An objective calling for eight months of heavy-up, October through May, is less desirable because it is too broad.

Reach/Frequency

Reach should be the primary objective nationally in order to provide broad coverage and to attract new customers. Frequency should be emphasized in the heavy-up areas, particularly in the East Central region where new competition is expected.

Note: The foregoing general goals are suggested by marketing objective 3. However, the marketing data do not provide adequate information to permit establishing specific reach and frequency goals.

Creative Implications

Select media that will permit visualization and simple product demonstrations.

Note: This objective should be broad enough to include both print and television. There is nothing in the copy platform that rules out the use of print.

Promotion Support

Provide media support for a sweepstakes promotion scheduled for January and a national couponing effort scheduled for October.

Note: This is an important objective because both promotions require media support, and the couponing effort rules out the exclusive use of broadcast media.

Merchandisability

To the extent possible, without jeopardizing the overall plan, select media that are merchandisable to the food store trade.

Note: This is not a vital objective, but it is strongly suggested because the company does not have its own sales force and must rely on brokers and wholesalers to sell and service the retail trade.

Budget

The foregoing media objectives are to be accomplished within a working media budget of $6,500,000.

Comments

In grading this assignment, the first five objectives should carry the most weight. Grades for the problem should be lowered if the objectives contain specific media choices.

Additional Assignments

Variations on this assignment can be developed by altering the bimonthly sales indices, regional sales indices, regional BDIs, or target audience information.

This assignment can also be used as a starting point from which students can develop a basic media strategy in which broad choices are made and justified. Some instructors might want to use it as the basis for the development of a complete media plan.

Planning Media Strategy

How to Use This Assignment

This is a take-home assignment because it takes time and thought to complete. It can be used as the major assignment in the course or as a preliminary assignment to the completion of an entire media plan. In fact, after a media strategy plan has been completed, you might want students to continue on the same problem and work out a complete plan.

The benefit of this assignment is that it does not take as much time as a complete plan would take, and yet most of the important media concepts can be found in the strategy.

What to Emphasize in Class

The foremost thing to emphasize is the problem-solving aspect of strategy. Students often approach media planning mechanically and fail to see that all of their decisions are related to problem solving. If students can create a logical and reasonable strategy based on a marketing situation, then they should have little trouble going on to complete a media plan.

Also emphasize the need to cover the most important decisions. To help them do this, ask them to read Assignment 28, the media plan checklist (II. Overall Strategy). Also note that media strategy *follows* media objectives.

One area of planning that bothers students is that of making decisions when there are few pertinent data to guide them. Students will have to use common sense and logic in this decision. Another area of difficulty is that of being able to support their decisions. That too is based on available research data, plus good judgment. The missing ingredient, of course, is experience, working under the direction of someone who really knows and understands media planning. The teacher's experiences and written material gathered from journals or trade publications like *Inside Media* magazine will have to be a substitute here.

Students will find it of value to calculate the percentages of sales by quarter to give them some guidance in setting the advertising budget by quarter. You might want to review the method of calculating these figures, which is detailed in point 6 of the answer to this assignment.

Students will find it helpful to consult the media rates information in the appendix as suggested in the problem discussion. Failure to have a reasonable idea of costs can result in a totally unrealistic plan.

Answer to Problem for Assignment 27

Media Strategies for the Media Objectives

1. *The primary target market will be women aged 14–24, with a secondary market of women aged 25–34.* The concentration should be on the younger group, especially the 14–17 group, who have a 400 BDI. The BDIs suggest that the strategic impressions be divided as follows:

Women aged 14–17   55%
Women aged 18–24   25%
Women aged 25–34   20%

Students might opt for even greater emphasis on the younger ages, perhaps 60/30/10. This could be justified by the marketing data and the idea that older women will not be as attracted to the tight-fitting style. (See Assignment 23 for further discussion of strategic impressions.)

2. *National coverage will be primarily through consumer magazines directed toward the target audience.* Magazines are selective and permit concentration on the target audience to a greater degree than other media. Magazines also provide excellent color reproduction, which seems essential for a stylish line of jeans that come in a variety of colors. Magazines such as *Seventeen* ($48,966 per four-color page), *'Teen* ($26,095), and *Cosmopolitan* ($69,170) reach the target audience at affordable rates. At an average cost of just over $48,000 per four-color page, a 12-insertion schedule in each magazine would cost about $1,731,000. Additional magazines could be added and spreads could be used during the peak selling seasons for a total magazine budget of under $3,000,000.

3. *Network, cable, and syndicated television will be used during the peak selling periods: August–September and December–January.* National TV will help provide needed heavy-up during peak seasons. The high cost of network TV precludes greater use of this medium, although cable and syndicated television can be used more extensively. It is important that students recognize the opportunities that cable and syndicated television provide to reach selected audiences at affordable rates. It is also important that students recognize that the budget for this brand will not allow year-long television advertising at effective levels.

4. *Network radio will be used to provide additional frequency during peak selling seasons.* Because magazines and television will be used as the primary media to provide visualization, radio can be added as a supplementary medium to increase frequency. Radio is also a medium that is heavily used by the primary target audience.

5. *Trade magazines directed to retailers of women's clothing will be used to fulfill the objective of maintaining strong communication with the retail trade.* Students might also recommend the use of direct mail to meet this objective. The important thing is that the need to communicate with the trade be recognized and provided for. Trade advertising is relatively inexpensive compared to consumer advertising. A trade budget of $200,000 should be sufficient.

6. *Suggested budget allocations by quarter.* Peak sales months are indicated in boldface type.

Third quarter (July, **August**, **September**)	33%
Fourth quarter (October, November, **December**)	28
First quarter (**January**, February, March)	22
Second quarter (April, May, June)	17

Using the seasonality of purchasing data reported under "Additional Marketing Information," budget allocations were calculated by adding the monthly indices for each quarter and then dividing the quarterly total by the yearly total as shown below.

Third quarter:	65 + 177 + 150 =	392
Fourth quarter:	81 + 79 + 169 =	329
First quarter:	120 + 75 + 69 =	264
Second quarter:	59 + 71 + 77 =	207
		1,192

Third quarter:	392 ÷ 1,192 = .32885 or	33%
Fourth quarter:	329 ÷ 1,192 = .27600 or	28
First quarter:	264 ÷ 1,192 = .22147 or	22
Second quarter:	207 ÷ 1,192 = .17365 or	17
		100%

Students might place even more emphasis on the peak selling months and drop all advertising during the second quarter of the year. The important thing is to place extra weight in periods when sales are above average.

7. *Media not used.* None of the local media (newspapers, spot television, spot radio, outdoor) were used because the media objectives did not indicate the need for spot media at this stage of the brand's launch. Also, due to the limited budget, diverting funds from national media for use in spot markets would weaken the national program. Finally, because the media objectives do not indicate what markets might benefit from additional advertising, it would be wise to wait until later when market-by-market sales data are available.

Additional reasons for not using certain media follow:

Newspapers.

- They do not reach the younger market very well.
- ROP color reproduction is poor.

Outdoor.

- Limited message length
- Low recall of messages

8. *Additional comments about the strategy.*
   - Magazines selected for this plan must be carefully chosen to ensure that the primary and secondary target audiences are reached as efficiently as possible. Magazines such as *Essence* and *Glamour* could certainly be added to those suggested in the first strategy point.

- Television programs—particularly network and syndicated programs—must be carefully selected to ensure efficient reach of the target market. MTV seems a logical cable network choice because it targets the teenage and young-adult market.
- Radio, while not providing visualization, is a very good supporting medium that can effectively and efficiently reach the primary target audience and build frequency. Also, by utilizing audio tracks adapted from the television commercials, radio commercials will reinforce the TV message each time they are heard.

Media Plan Checklist

How to Use This Assignment

This is really an assignment that should accompany a media plan that you give to your class. Its purpose is simply to help students remember what is necessary to include in a written planning assignment. If you do not assign a media plan, then you might want students to study each of the items on the checklist simply to have them know what is essential in a written plan.

What to Emphasize in Class

A media plan document is much like a plan of battle in warfare or a blueprint for a building. It offers direction for action. But it also offers a means of control. Once a specific course of action is explained, then a planner can control the outcome of such action to whatever effect he or she wants to occur.

So here are some ideas to emphasize in class:

* A complete media plan must be based on marketing information summarized or presented somewhere else. Sometimes the marketing objectives and strategies are placed immediately in front of a plan document. Other times they are kept separate.

* Rationales can often be summarized in a written document, but planners must be able to defend their decisions orally upon request if it is not done in writing. Space often does not permit more than a sentence or two in defense of any decision. But when planners appear in a meeting, someone might ask them to explain in detail why they chose a particular approach. Therefore, planners' rationale must be strong and complete. A sketchy, superficial rationale often causes others to suspect the plan is not adequate.

* Not all media plans are alike, and it is possible that for a specialized product in a specialized marketing situation, all of the checklist items will not be necessary. There are exceptions to most rules.

* Despite the fact that students can check every detail on this checklist, they might have poorly presented plans if their presentation techniques are poor. Failure to place headlines on tables or failure to identify sources of information often harm an otherwise good plan. A good presentation document is orderly, logical, and concise.

Media Strategy Planning Problem
National Support of a Product on a Small Budget

How to Use This Assignment

This assignment asks students to develop complete media strategy recommendations, but not detailed plan tactics. Thus, you will probably want to use this as a take-home assignment. You might wish to have students continue on the same problem and work out a complete plan.

Because a detailed plan is not required, you might wish to use this assignment for in-class discussion after students have completed their analysis and homework on this problem.

What to Emphasize in Class

Advise students to consider carefully the marketing and media objectives to make sure that their strategies are all directed toward meeting the objectives. Also, advise students that they should review the discussion questions at the end of the assignment before developing strategies. The discussion questions were developed to help students think about media opportunities and problems associated with this case.

Students are not required to develop complete plan tactics, but it will be necessary for them to consider media costs to make sure that any recommended strategy will be workable. There is no use considering media that are unaffordable. You might also review how to compute CPM for media audiences so students can use this analysis to select the most efficient vehicles in each class.

Encourage students to provide detailed rationales to support their strategy recommendations. You might also ask them to indicate their reasons for *not* using certain media alternatives.

Advise students that they are to refer to the media costs listed in the appendix and the spot TV costs listed in Exhibit 32–1 as they develop their strategies. Because trade communication is a specific marketing and media objective, costs and circulations for selected trade magazines are included in Table 29–1 in the assignment. Students are free to recommend any of the media classes/vehicles for which they have cost data. Also remind them to review the MRI data on adhesive bandage users as shown in Exhibit 29–1. These data will help them evaluate media classes and vehicles.

Answers to Problems for Assignment 29

1. Considering the size of the budget, it is unlikely that year-long continuity can be achieved. Any attempt to spread the available media dollars over the entire year would result in weight levels too low to accomplish objectives.

   On a limited budget, it would be wise to concentrate the budget during the peak usage season—May through September. This five-month period seems to be the maximum length of time that adequate weight levels can be maintained. October is not included because the seasonal trend indicates that usage declines when children are back in school, and it can be assumed that the 105 index for September–October is due to above-average usage in September that balances below-average usage in October.

The brand needs a strong kick-off in May (note the planned couponing effort), so it would seem appropriate to maintain heaviest weights at the beginning of the peak season and allow weights to decrease somewhat toward the end of the season (August and September).

2. The marketing and media objectives call for additional weight in areas where product sales are highest. This certainly indicates the use of spot media to heavy-up key markets. The data available are limited and do not include market-by-market sales information. However, students do know sales by Nielsen territory and also that sales tend to be higher in metropolitan markets. Based on this information, it would be logical to establish criteria requiring that selected spot markets be located in Nielsen territories with indices above 100 and be among the top 50 markets in size. This would restrict spot markets to those top 50 markets located in Nielsen's West Central and Pacific territories. Although not precise, this approach is supportable and is certainly better than arbitrarily selecting markets.

3. The media objectives certainly indicate the need to use broadcast media in order to properly present the jingle commercials. Also, because the promotion objectives require media support of a coupon drop in May, some print media must be used.

Recommended Media Strategy

There are several approaches to this problem. Given the same media planning problem, no two media planners will come up with identical plans. Here is one solution.

1. Use a media mix of daytime network television, early fringe spot television in 14 key markets, three national magazines, and three trade magazines (one to cover each class-of-trade).
   a. Daytime network was chosen because it is cost efficient, and daytime has significantly above-average index numbers among heavy users of adhesive bandages (127 and 113). Network TV provides the national coverage that is called for and also provides a vehicle to carry the jingle commercials. Fifty GRPs per week will be scheduled for 11 weeks during the peak selling season.
   b. Spot television is used in the 14 top-50 markets that are located in the West Central and Pacific regions. Spot TV provides the needed heavy-up in key markets and also provides a vehicle to carry the jingle commercials. Fifty GRPs will be scheduled for 10 weeks during early fringe time. Early fringe will increase reach in the key markets to help attract new users. Also, early fringe has a 111 index among heavy users.
   c. Three national consumer magazines will be used in May to provide vehicles to carry coupons. Magazines with high reach of users and good cost efficiency were chosen: *Family Circle, Woman's Day,* and *Reader's Digest.*

d. Three trade magazines were selected, each one covering a different class-of-trade. Four, 4-color pages (7" × 10" ads in tabloids) are scheduled in each publication. The additional cost for color was considered worthwhile because color will help gain attention and increase memorability for Acme brand. Ads will be scheduled beginning in March issues to encourage advance stocking of the product and later during the campaign to encourage continued stocking.

2. The following spot television markets were selected:

Market	Region	% U.S. HH	C/RP Early Fringe
1. Los Angeles	Pacific	5.2	$ 405
2. Chicago	West Central	3.3	175
3. San Francisco	Pacific	2.4	257
4. Minneapolis–St. Paul	West Central	1.5	85
5. Seattle–Tacoma	Pacific	1.5	114
6. St. Louis	West Central	1.2	54
7. Sacramento–Stockton	Pacific	1.2	85
8. Phoenix	Pacific	1.2	82
9. Denver	West Central	1.2	87
10. San Diego	Pacific	1.0	118
11. Portland, OR	Pacific	.9	71
12. Milwaukee	West Central	.8	50
13. Kansas City	West Central	.8	50
14. Salt Lake City	Pacific	.7	77
		23.0	$1,710

3. Consumer magazines selected were as follows:

Magazine	% Reach users	User reach (000)	Cost (Four-color page)	CPM users
Reader's Digest	32.8%	19,094	151,900	7.96
Family Circle	24.5	14,286	96,990	6.79
Woman's Day	23.2	13,512	84,320	6.24

4. Trade magazines selected were as follows:

Magazine	Circulation	Cost (Four-color page)	CPM
Supermarket Business	70,387	14,595	207.35
American Druggist	92,135	8,400	91.17
Discount Merchandiser	34,851	10,500	301.28

Trade magazines were selected based on cost-per-thousand analysis. This is an oversimplification, but it is a reasonable criterion. An analysis of circulation by geographic area and business classification would be appropriate additional criteria if such information were available to students.

5. Recommended scheduling places heaviest weight during the introductory months, and weight decreases as the season progresses.

Weeks	March 1 2 3 4	April 1 2 3 4	May 1 2 3 4	June 1 2 3 4	July 1 2 3 4	August 1 2 3 4	September 1 2 3 4
Network TV 50 HH GRP/week Daytime 11 weeks			X X X	X X X	X X	X X	X
Spot TV 50 HH GRP/week Fringe 10 weeks			X X X	X X X	X X	X X	
Consumer magazines			XXXXXXX				
Trade magazines	XXXXXXX	XXXXXXX		XXXXXXX		XXXXXXX	

6. Budget allocations break down as follows:

Vehicle	Cost	% of Total
Network TV	$2,127,000	60.8
Spot TV	855,000	24.4
Consumer magazines	333,210	9.5
Trade magazines	133,980	3.8
Reserve	50,810	1.5
	$3,500,000	100.0

Month	Cost	% of Total
March	$ 33,495	1.0
April	33,495	1.0
May	1,257,210	36.4
June	957,495	27.8
July	487,800	14.1
August	521,295	15.1
September	158,400	4.6
	$3,449,190*	100.0

*Does not include $50,810 reserve.

7. Radio was not used because, although it provides a vehicle to carry the jingle commercials, it does not have the visual impact of television. Using television *and* radio would spread the budget too thinly over two media. Had there been sufficient budget, radio might have been used as a supplemental medium to increase frequency.

8. Cable TV was not recommended because it would not provide the national coverage of network television. Currently, cable is in just over 65 percent of all U.S. television homes. Cable might be used on a local basis as part of the spot TV plan.

How a Professional Media Planner Solved a Marketing/Media Problem
An Annotated Media Plan for Lux Liquid

How to Use This Assignment

Adequate time should be devoted to study and review of this case problem/solution, which provides a rather complete discussion of a media plan recommendation. This discussion should help the student who does not understand how the various steps to a media plan fit together or who needs to learn how to develop a more complete rationale for media plan recommendations.

Students should review this media problem and recommendation only after they have a reasonably thorough understanding of basic media planning considerations presented in this workbook and the media planning course.

You might use this for in-class discussion; students could use it for review before completion of a major media plan project; or you might ask students to develop an alternative media plan approach to the one presented in this assignment. (See comments at end of this discussion.)

What to Emphasize in Class

Encourage students to review workbook comments on the objectives and approach suggested for this assignment, as well as the statement of the problem that confronted the professional planner. This will encourage the student to review the solution more carefully.

Note the organization of the solution, namely, discussion of marketing objectives and situation, media objectives, media strategy statements, discussion of tactics by medium, additional media considerations, backup data charts, media schedule, and budget comparisons. Ask students what "roll-out," "positioning," and "defense tactics" mean.

Remind the students that although an extensive discussion of the recommendation is presented, various charts and backup data have been omitted due to space limitations within the workbook. Obviously, the thorough media planner will be prepared with additional data charts and rationale to answer specific questions that arise during the approval process.

Note that the media planner was willing to question marketing objectives and to suggest specific implications for the media plan.

Spend time on the discussion, asking students for alternatives and discussing whether these alternatives are as viable as those the planner offered.

The statement of media objectives covers most of the considerations outlined in Assignment 26. Statements of media strategy concisely state basic media approaches recommended and the major reason or value of each strategy approach. Detailed discussion of the media plan is provided under discussion of plan tactics. (Although "media objectives" and "media strategy" are frequently used as headings in media plans and presentations, "plan tactics" is not a standard heading for all media plan presentations.)

Some students will think that only heavy users should be targets, others that medium and light users will be more brand loyal to Lux, and others that all users should be the base for analysis. Obviously, if Lux is to achieve the stated marketing objectives, a broader base is needed than heavy users. If heavy users are omitted, chances for major volume gains are greatly diminished. A further refinement is special emphasis to the medium/heavy user who does not currently use Lux.

Other key plan considerations are strong initial effort, concentration of media effort in television, heavy-up effort in high-potential and opportunity markets, and budget flexibility.

The following indicates how the tables are to be read:

- **Table 30–1.** Homemakers aged 18–24 account for 13.0 percent of heavy/medium users (this is 5 percent lower than incidence of heavy/medium users among all homemakers). Incidence of heavy/medium users and non-Lux users in this age segment is 3 percent above average against all homemakers. This age segment was considered secondary in importance to the 35–49 age segment.

- **Table 30–2.** Of heavy/medium and non-Lux users, 37.6 percent view daytime network TV (incidence of day TV viewing is 17 percent greater than for all homemakers).

  CPM for user households in day net TV is $.92. With only one non-Lux and heavy/medium user for every four "viewing" sets (ratio of .24), CPM for this usage category of viewer is $3.83. If day CPM is considered the base for comparison, then early news CPM for this usage category is 25 percent greater than for day TV.

- **Table 30–3.** Dollars spent for Lux are compared with the major competitor Ivory and with all competitors. (Certain assumptions were made about how budget allocations should be calculated. These assumptions are listed on page XXX.)

- **Table 30–4.** At 205 GRP/week (stated in household GRP), at a rate of 145 GRP/week in day and 60 GRP/week in fringe, 88 percent of all TV households are reached over a four-week period at an average frequency of 9.5 times. Over the four-week period, 64 percent of TV households will be reached four or more times, 18 percent will be reached two to three times, and only 6 percent will be reached with only one exposure.

- **Tables 30–5.** Lux plan calls for 2,200 GRP weight level for national coverage during first quarter and 2,640 GRP weight level in spot markets for the same period.

Comments

One can never state all considerations that support a media plan recommendation. However, this is probably the most comprehensive and thorough discussion of media plan considerations available for review.

It should be noted that the original presentation of the media recommendation (with four-color slides and deeper explanation of more numbers than presented here) was well received by professional media planners at the *Ad Age* Media Workshop.

As a note to students who think this is the only acceptable media recommendation or approach for this problem, it should be mentioned that another respected professional media planner presented a different plan (with different TV daypart emphasis), and it too was well received at the workshop. Obviously, given different assumptions, media planners will develop different recommendations. However, both of these presentations were backed with solid reasoning and strong presentation of logic and support data—the hallmark of excellent media planning.

Section Four

Miscellaneous Problems

Developing a Complete Media Plan

How to Use This Assignment

This is a take-home assignment because it requires substantial time and thought. It should be used as a major assignment or, if you wish, as a basis for in-class discussion of a media planning problem prior to completion of another major project.

What to Emphasize in Class

The $8.0 million media budget for this brand is not considered especially large for a packaged food product. Note the much higher spending levels reported in the assignment for Healthy Choice and Lean Cuisine. However, $8.0 million is considered to be an adequate budget for a specialty food item.

Review with students the assignments dealing with writing media objectives (Assignment 26) and media strategies (Assignments 27 and 29). Point out the need to carefully review the marketing background prior to deciding on media objectives and strategies. You might want to have students turn in these portions of the plan for preliminary grading before they continue. This will give you an opportunity to point out any obvious errors or omissions that could adversely affect the overall plan.

Here are some items to consider when grading this assignment. You might want to point out these items to your students.

1. The plan should take into account the seasonality of the product category. There is certainly adequate data to justify increased weights during above-average usage months.

2. Students should carefully select markets for additional advertising emphasis. Although market-by-market sales data are not provided, there are two clues to market selection: (1) the brand's above-average performance in the Middle Atlantic and West Central regions and (2) the fact that the brand enjoys strength in metro areas of A and B counties. This certainly suggests emphasis on the top 50 markets that are located in the Middle Atlantic and West Central areas.

3. Costs should be based on those available in the appendix and in Assignments 32 (spot TV) and 29 (Grocery Trade Magazines). Of course, if students have access to SRDS, you could opt to have them use that cost data. Using SRDS gives students a wider choice of magazine space units.

4. The assignment points out that the brand has a very small sales force, and the marketing objectives call for strong communication with the food store trade. Students should be aware of the importance of trade communication and should include media objectives that call for it and media strategies that provide for it.

5. In making media selections, point out that if magazines are being used, specific magazines (both consumer and trade) should be recommended. In

the case of broadcast, the recommendations should center on the day-part(s) to be used. Television recommendations could also include program types (but not specific programs), and radio recommendations should specify network(s) to be used and/or station formats in the case of spot radio. The MRI data included in this assignment provide data to support media selection recommendations. Suggest to students that from this data they can develop CPM figures based on dieters reached by each magazine, which is much more specific than using circulation or rate base information for CPM calculations.

6. In the case of broadcast recommendations, review how to use cost per rating point (C/RP) data to estimate both television and radio costs. This principle is covered in Assignment 32 on spot TV planning. The same principle applies to network TV planning, and network C/RP by quarter by daypart is provided in the appendix.

7. Point out to students the need to compute reach and frequency figures for both the national effort and for the key markets that will receive added weight. Both sets of figures should be shown either on the schedule spreadsheet or in a separate table.

Answer to Problem for Assignment 31

What follows is a possible solution to the media planning problem presented in this assignment. Other planners would come up with different recommendations or at least with variations on this plan. However, the plan is a viable solution to the problem.

Media Objectives

1. **Target audience.** Direct messages to dieters, primarily college-educated female homemakers aged 25–54. (It is important to indicate the need to reach dieters as data are provided that help to pinpoint media usage by dieters. It is also important to recognize that dieting females are the primary targets.)

2. **Regionality.** Provide national coverage to support national distribution and sales. Also, provide additional weight in top 50 markets in the Middle Atlantic and West Central regions where sales are above average. (This objective should include both the need for national coverage and the need to place extra weight in the Middle Atlantic and West Central regions where sales are above average.)

3. **Seasonality.** While year-long continuity is desirable, it is more important to provide adequate weight during the peak sales period from April through August. It is also important to place heavier emphasis at the beginning of the season (April and May) to provide a strong kick-off to the advertising/marketing effort. (It is important that students recognize the need to have a strong kick-off and that emphasis be placed on the peak sales months.)

4. **Reach/frequency.** Nationally emphasize reach to attract new customers while maintaining a minimum 2.5 frequency. Increase frequency in key markets to help consolidate the brand's sales position. (Students might come up with a different minimum frequency level; however, the important

thing is to indicate that reach/frequency emphasis will be different nationally than it will be in the spot markets.)

5. **Creative implications.** Primary media should provide for visualization of the product. (There is little in the case to suggest any specific media choices. By specifying visualization for primary media, the objective still would allow radio to be used as a secondary or supporting medium.)

6. **Promotion support.** Provide media to support the coupon drop scheduled for March and the sweepstakes planned for July. (Because these promotions have been scheduled, the plan must recognize the need to support them.)

7. **Trade communication.** Provide media to direct messages to the retail food trade to encourage stocking and promotion of the brand. (This is an important objective called for by the marketing objectives. Students might opt to include this as an additional target audience under objective 1.)

8. **Merchandisability.** To the extent possible, without jeopardizing the effectiveness of the plan, select media that are merchandisable to the retail trade. (This is not a vital objective, but it is certainly warranted by the fact that the brand has a small sales force and the marketing objectives call for trade communication and the need to expand distribution.)

9. **Budget.** The foregoing objectives are to be accomplished within a working media budget of $8,000,000. (It is always a good idea to spell out the budget constraint in the objectives.)

Media Strategies

1. Use four-color pages in national consumer magazines to provide national coverage, attractive visual presentation of the product, and to support the coupon and sweepstakes efforts.

2. Use trade magazines directed to food retailers to maintain communication with the trade and to inform the trade of promotions and advertising efforts supporting the brand.

3. Use a combination of early morning and early evening news on network television to dramatically present the product and to help generate national reach.

4. Use spot television in daytime and news programs in 13 of the top 50 markets to increase weight levels in those key markets in the Middle Atlantic and West Central regions.

5. Kick off the campaign in March—the beginning of the peak usage season— and continue advertising throughout the above-average usage period.

Magazine Selection

Initially, the magazines listed in Exhibit 31–1 were examined. The eight with both high reach of dieters and high index numbers (above 120) received further analysis. Magazine groups were not included because costs for combinations and groups are not included in the appendix. The eight selected follow:

Magazine	Reach of dieters (%)	Index
Better Homes & Gardens	21.5%	121
Family Circle	18.9	137
Good Housekeeping	18.7	129
Ladies' Home Journal	14.1	134
McCall's	13.3	135
Modern Maturity	23.5	128
Redbook	9.0	130
Woman's Day	16.3	132

From this group of eight, four magazines were selected based on their CPM for total audience and CPM for dieters, as shown in the following table:

Magazine	Total audience (000)	Dieters (000)	Cost (four-color page)	CPM audience	CPM dieters
*Better Homes & Gardens	31,746	12,307	147,500	4.65	11.99
*Family Circle	24,628	10,845	96,990	3.94	8.94
*Good Housekeeping	25,743	10,684	122,035	4.35	10.49
Ladies' Home Journal	18,825	8,103	92,100	4.89	11.37
McCall's	17,548	7,593	83,315	4.75	10.97
Modern Maturity	32,797	13,481	226,970	6.92	16.84
Redbook	12,278	5,143	69,755	5.68	13.56
*Woman's Day	21,978	9,313	84,320	3.84	9.05

*Magazines selected.

Although *McCall's* and *Ladies' Home Journal* have a lower CPM for dieters than *Better Homes & Gardens,* they have lower reach and a higher CPM for total audience. For these reasons, *Better Homes & Gardens* was selected over *McCall's* and *Ladies' Home Journal.*

Television Daypart Selection
A review of the employment status of dieters in Exhibit 31–1 indicates that 63.4 percent are employed full time (55.8 percent) or part time (7.6 percent). As a result, it was determined that daytime would be the lowest cost daypart, but it would have to be supplemented with another time period to help ensure reach of working dieters. Exhibit 31–1 also indicates that early morning (index 108) and early fringe (index 105) are popular dayparts with dieters. Further, it indicates that among the most popular program types with dieters are early morning talk/info/news shows (index 123) and early evening network news (index 118). Based on these findings, a combination of daytime (early morning) and early evening news is recommended for network television. The budget will not permit the use of prime-time network television at adequate weight levels. The same daypart combination (daytime and news) is recommended in the spot TV markets.

Spot Television Market Selection
In keeping with the marketing background and the marketing objectives, spot TV markets were selected based on size and location. Markets selected had to be located in the regions with above-average sales indices—Middle Atlantic (113) and West Central (117)—and they had to be among the 50 largest markets in the United States. Following these criteria, 13 markets covering 24 percent of U.S. television households were selected, as follows:

ADI market	Region	TV HH (%)
New York	Middle Atlantic	7.0
Chicago	West Central	3.3
Philadelphia	Middle Atlantic	2.8
Washington, DC	Middle Atlantic	2.0
Minneapolis–St. Paul	West Central	1.5
St. Louis	West Central	1.2
Denver	West Central	1.2
Baltimore	Middle Atlantic	1.2
Milwaukee	West Central	.8
Kansas City	West Central	.8
Buffalo	Middle Atlantic	.7
Harrisburg–York–Lancaster	Middle Atlantic	.6
Wilkes Barre–Scranton	Middle Atlantic	.6
		23.5

Lacking market-by-market sales and share information, this method of market selection was believed to be appropriate, and it is certainly better than arbitrarily selecting spot markets. Another planner might have extended the size criteria from the top 50 markets to the top 60 or 75 markets. Lacking specific information, this is a subjective decision. For purposes of this plan, the top 50 markets represent the large metropolitan markets where the brand would be most likely to have strong sales.

Trade Magazine Selection
Of the three food trade magazines available, the two with the lowest CPM were chosen. Although this should not necessarily be the only criterion, it is a reasonable one, and additional data for making a decision were not available. Considering the importance of maintaining communication with the retail trade, the use of two publications and six full-page, four-color insertions in each was justified. The most important consideration, however, should be that students realize the need for trade communication and that they select at least one trade publication.

Publication	Circulation (000)	Cost (four-color page)	CPM
Progressive Grocer	63.7	$13,860	$217.58
*Supermarket Business	70.4	14,595	207.32
*Supermarket News	51.7	10,800	208.90

*Publications selected.

Scheduling Rationale
The bimonthly sales indices indicate that above-average sales of the brand begin in early spring and run through the summer months. Because the budget will not permit yearlong advertising at adequate weight levels, the decision was made to concentrate the available funds during the peak selling season—March through August. By concentrating the budget in a shorter period of time, adequate reach and frequency levels can be achieved. This was thought to be a better approach than spreading the budget over an entire year and never really developing adequate weight levels.

In keeping with the marketing objectives, the heaviest schedules are placed in March and April to provide a strong introductory effort. The heaviest schedules of magazine ads are in March to provide a distribution vehicle for coupons and again in June to support the planned sweepstakes promotion.

Note that trade magazine ads are scheduled beginning in January to lead the season and to urge retail stocking prior to the campaign kick-off in March. Students should understand that trade advertising must lead the consumer program by six to eight weeks to provide adequate time for retail stocking.

The schedule flowchart shows how all the media have been scheduled.

Reach/Frequency Calculations

Remind students that reach and frequency calculations required on the flowchart should be figured separately for national and spot markets. Spot market reach and frequency will always be higher than the national reach and frequency because the spot markets receive spot weight in addition to the national media weight. It would be misleading to show only the combined spot market reach and frequency, especially when the spot markets account for only 24 percent of the U.S. households.

The reach and frequency calculations shown on the flowchart were calculated using the tables in Assignment 16 and the magazine audience figures contained in Exhibit 31–1. Figures were combined using the Sainsbury formula (Assignment 17). Here is how the March figures were calculated:

Magazines	Audience (Exhibit 31–1)		Universe (Exhibit 31–1)	Reach (%)
Better Homes & Gardens	31,746	÷	178,281	= .178 or 17.8%
Family Circle	24,628	÷	178,281	= .138 or 13.8
Good Houskeeping	25,743	÷	178,281	= .144 or 14.4
Woman's Day	21,978	÷	178,281	= .123 or 12.3

The monthly frequency for each magazine is 1, so the GRPs are 58.3 (17.8 + 13.8 + 14.4 + 12.3 = 58.3). Using Sainsbury, the combined reach for the four magazines is 44 percent:

$$(1.00-.178) \times (1.00-.138) \times (1.00-.144) \times (1.00-.123) =$$
$$.822 \times .862 \times .856 \times .877 = .53 \text{ (non-reach) or 47\% reach}$$

Then, reducing the reach figure by 7 percent (because four vehicles were combined) results in a final estimated reach of 44 percent (47 × .93 = 43.7).

Network TV. Interpolating from Table 16–1, 150 GRPs split between daytime and early news would be about 51 percent.

Spot TV. Interpolating from Table 16–2, 150 GRPs split between daytime and fringe would be about 47 percent.

National reach and frequency. Again, using Sainsbury to combine magazine and network TV to get national reach and frequency results in a combined reach of 74 percent:

$(1.00-.51) \times (1.00-.44) = .49 \times .56 = .27$ (non-reach) or 73% reach

Frequency is 2.9.
Magazine GRPs = 58.3
Network GRPs = 150.0
$208.3 \div 73 = 2.85$ or 2.9

Spot market reach and frequency. To figure spot market reach and frequency, the spot TV reach must be combined with the national reach using Sainsbury.

Magazine reach = 44%
Network reach = 51
Spot TV reach = 47

$(1.00-.44) \times (1.00-.51) \times (1.00-.47) =$
$.56 \times .49 \times .53 = .145$ (non-reach) or 85.5 reach.
Reducing that reach figure by 5 percent because three vehicles were combined results in an estimated spot market reach of 81 percent. ($85.5 \times .95 = .81$).

Spot market frequency is 4.4.

Magazine GRPs = 58.3
Network GRPs = 150.0
Spot TV GRPs = 150.0
$358.3 \div 81 = 4.42$ or 4.4

Budget recap

Medium	Cost ($)	Percentage of Total
Consumer magazines	$1,322,535	16.5%
Network television	5,368,400	67.1
Spot television	1,015,125	12.7
Trade magazines	152,370	1.9
Reserve	141,570	1.8
Total	$8,000,000	100.0%

Detailed budget breakdown

Magazines
Better Homes & Gardens—3, 4/c pages @ 147,500 ... 442,500
Family Circle—3, 4/c pages @ 96,990 290,970
Good Housekeeping—3, 4/c pages @ 112,035 336,105
Woman's Day—3, 4/c pages @ 84,320 252,960
 $1,322,535

Network television
Early morning—March: 75 GRPs @ 6,213 465,975
Early news—March: 75 GRPs @ 7,207 540,525
Early morning—April/May/June: 200 GRPs @ 6,655 1,331,000
Early news—April/May/June: 200 GRPs @ 9,272 ... 1,845,400
Early morning—July/August: 100 GRPs @ 5,150 ... 515,000
Early news—July/August: 100 GRPs @ 6,615 661,500
 5,368,400

Spot television*

New York—750 GRPs @ 370.50	277,875
Chicago—750 GRPs @ 178	133,500
Philadelphia—750 GRPs @ 150	112,500
Washington, DC—750 GRPs @ 129.50	97,125
Minneapolis–St. Paul—750 GRPs @ 98	73,500
St. Louis—750 GRPs @ 56	42,000
Denver—750 GRPs @ 66.50	49,875
Baltimore—750 GRPs @ 75	56,250
Milwaukee—750 GRPs @ 60.50	45,375
Kansas City—750 GRPs @ 53	39,750
Buffalo—750 GRPs @ 37	27,750
Harrisburg–York–Lancaster—750 GRPs @ 50.50 ...	37,875
Wilkes Barre–Scranton—750 GRPs @ 29	21,750
	1,015,125

*Each market figured at 750 GRPs (50 per week for 15 weeks—25 GRPs in daytime and 25 GRPs in news). C/RP is average of early morning and early news.

Trade magazines

Supermarket News—6, 4/c pages @ 10,800	64,800
Supermarket Business—6, 4/c pages @ 14,595	87,570
	152,370
Reserve:	141,570
Total:	$8,000,000

Note: A month-by-month breakdown of the budget is included on the schedule flowchart.

Exhibit 31–2   Advertising Flowchart

	Jan.	Feb.	Mar.	Apr.	May	June	July	Aug.	Sept.	Oct.	Nov.	Dec.	Total
Week													
MAGAZINES PAGE, 4/C													
B H & G													
FAMILY CIR.													
G. HOUSEKPG.													
WOMAN'S DAY													
NET TV													
E. MORN 25 GRP													
E. NEWS 25 GRP													
SPOT TV													
DAYTIME 25 GRP													
E. NEWS 25 GRP													
TRADE MAGS. PAGE, 4/C													
SUPERMKT.NEWS													
SUPERMKT.BUS.													
* Monthly REACH			74	64	53	58	70	45					
* Monthly FREQUENCY			2.9	2.8	2.2	2.8	2.3	2.2					
* SPOT MKT.R/F			81/4.4	77/4.3	69/3.1	74/4.2	78/3.3	68/2.9					
Dollars per mo. (000)	25.4	25.4	1675.8	1629.4	1054.1	1535.0	1164.5	749.0					7858.6
Budget monthly (%)	.3	.3	21.3	20.7	13.4	19.5	14.8	9.5					99.8**

*Does not include Trade Magazines.

**Due to rounding.

Spot TV Planning

How to Use This Assignment

Considering the number of calculations needed to complete this assignment, it is probably best to use it as a take-home assignment. You can, of course, discuss the solutions in class following completion of the assignment at home.

What to Emphasize in Class

In addition to the material covered in the discussion of this assignment, several areas should be stressed in class.

First, it is important that students understand that most spot TV planning and budgeting is done on the basis of estimated cost per rating point in each market. Agencies and advertisers rarely plan on the basis of the cost per commercial, except in the case of local advertisers dealing directly with TV stations.

The larger agencies and major national advertisers often compute their own cost per rating point based on their experience with actual buys in each market. Lacking in-house cost-per-rating-point information, smaller agencies and advertisers can use data supplied by several companies. One company is Spot Quotations and Data (SQAD), which supplied the data used in this assignment. SQAD analyzes data supplied by cooperating agencies and publishes monthly reports on estimated costs per GRP. Although the cost-per-point data presented in this assignment is for TV households, SQAD also can provide cost-per-rating-point data for various demographic groups, such as women aged 25–54. SQAD data are available on computer disk/tape as well as in printed form.

Point out that GRP goals are usually set in multiples of 5 (e.g., 50, 55, 60). Students should be discouraged from setting GRP goals such as 53 or 64.

When making this assignment, you might want to clarify one of the guidelines listed under "Problem." The reference to "good continuity throughout the 13-week period" in point d assumes that each market will receive the same number of weeks of advertising and that the goal is to maximize the number of weeks. Some students might develop a rather complex schedule in which some markets receive ten weeks of advertising, others eleven, some twelve, etc. This should be discouraged unless there is justification for such scheduling. If there is no real justification, this complex scheduling merely complicates the problem and will also complicate the making of the actual buy.

Answers to Problems for Assignment 32

1.

Market	Cost/GRP	GRP/week	Cost/week	Number of weeks	Cost
Philadelphia	$150	90	$13,500	13	$175,500
Boston	183	90	16,470	13	214,110
Detroit	92	90	8,280	13	107,640
Atlanta	92	90	8,280	13	107,640
Seattle–Tacoma	114	60	6,840	13	88,920
Tampa–St. Petersburg	85	60	5,100	13	66,300
Miami	135	60	8,100	13	105,300
Nashville	46	60	2,720	13	35,880
Kansas City	50	60	3,000	13	39,000
					$940,290

Note that the established budget will permit 13 weeks of advertising at GRP levels above the minimum.

2.

Market	Cost/GRP	GRP/week	Cost/week	Number of weeks	Cost
Philadelphia	$236	75	$17,700	10	$177,000
Boston	285	75	21,375	10	213,750
Detroit	121	75	9,075	10	90,750
Atlanta	130	75	9,750	10	97,500
Seattle–Tacoma	144	50	7,200	10	72,000
Tampa–St. Petersburg	140	50	7,000	10	70,000
Miami	208	50	10,400	10	104,000
Nashville	90	50	4,500	10	45,000
Kansas City	95	50	4,750	10	47,500
					$917,500

Recommended scheduling of the ten weeks of advertising:

Four weeks of advertising
One-week hiatus
Three weeks of advertising
One-week hiatus
Three weeks of advertising

Note that the only way to stay within budget and provide the maximum number of weeks of advertising is to use minimum GRP levels for ten weeks. Higher GRP levels would result in fewer weeks of advertising, which would not meet the objective of maximizing the number of weeks of heavy-up. Students should be discouraged from increasing the number of weeks in one or two markets just to use up the budget. The problem calls for 50 percent more weight in high sales markets but provides no further justification for treating one market differently from the others.

Additional Assignments

A number of different assignments can be developed using the source material provided in Exhibit 32–1. Merely vary the GRP levels, budget, markets, and/or daypart to be used.

Allocating an Advertising Budget to Spot TV Markets

How to Use This Assignment

The purpose of this assignment is, primarily, to bring about understanding about a widely used spot TV allocator. But there is also the possibility that if students have a computer and a spreadsheet program, they can use this assignment as a first step in knowing how much to spend in spot TV markets.

What to Emphasize in Class

Emphasize, most of all, the fact that network television does not deliver ratings directly proportional to sales in any given market. A network TV program could have a 25 national rating but only a 10 rating in market *X*, one of the best markets. Therefore, there is a need to compensate for this weakness. Also tell students that this is a form of "weighting" by which the dollars allocated are related to a market's sales potential. Weighting is a technique of achieving larger audiences in local markets that have better sales potential.

Emphasize the idea of a pro-rata advertising budget. This idea might surprise students who think that we ought to put more money in weak markets in order to build them up. That technique is risky because your brand has to overcome the power of well-established brands. A safer technique is to place money in a market where you know your brand sells well.

This technique also is important because it helps explain how advertising works. Advertising cannot sell any product to everyone. It sells best to those who already have purchased a product, or people who are demographically or psychographically like those who have already purchased.

Make sure that students understand the function of index numbers as used here. Indices are a way to have a computer quickly find the most overdelivered market in a long list of markets. An index number shows a relationship. Finally, emphasize the fact that BDIs are often used instead of sales by market in using this technique.

Answer to Problem for Assignment 33

Note that it is important for students to know how every calculation was made, or they might miss important aspects of the solution.

Market	Percent of sales	Network delivery	Pro-rata budget	Index	Adjusted network budget	Spot TV budget
A	15%	19%	$375,000[b]	127	$296,875	$ 78,125
B	10	7	250,000	70	109,375	140,625
C	30	23	750,000	77	359,375	390,625
D	15	11	375,000	73	171,875	203,125
E	20	24	500,000	120	375,000	125,000
F	10	16[a]	250,000	160	250,000	0
	100%	100%	$2,500,000		$1,562,500[a]	$937,500

[a] $\chi (.16) = \$250,000$; $\chi = \$1,562,500$
[b] $.15 \times \$2,500,000 = \$375,000$

Spot TV Buying Problem

How to Use This Assignment

Because of the analysis needed to properly evaluate spot TV availabilities, this is best used as a take-home assignment. You might want to discuss the buys in class after the students have completed their work at home.

What to Emphasize in Class

This assignment has been simplified to make it easier for students to handle. You should point out that in actual practice the buyer would work up his or her own audience estimates rather than relying on data provided by the station representative. (See Assignment 14.) Also, the costs for most TV spots are negotiable, and negotiating is an important function of the buyer.

Many students are not familiar with the role of the TV station representative in spot buying situations. You will probably want to discuss this with students and, if possible, invite a rep and/or buyer to talk to your class.

Some other things you might want to cover in class are the following:

- The CPM for daytime programs will usually be lower than for fringe programs.

- The CPM for women aged 25–54 impressions is calculated by dividing the weekly cost times 1,000 by the total women aged 25–54 impressions.

Answer to Problem for Assignment 34

Station	Day	Time	Program	DMA rating	Total women (000)	Women 25–54 (000)	Cost	CPM women 25–54
WIS–TV	M–F	9–11A	Regis/Kathy Lee[a]	8	19	10	$ 70	7.00
WIS–TV	M–F	9–11A	Regis/Kathy Lee[a]	8	19	10	70	7.00
WIS–TV	Sat.	1130P	Saturday Night Live	8	16	12	125	10.42
WOLO–TV	M–F	1–4P	Day Rotation	9	24	18	130	7.22
WOLO–TV	M–F	11P	News	11	20	14	150	10.71
WACH–TV	M–F	1–2P	Sally Jesse Raphael	5	15	10	80	8.00
WACH–TV	M–F	6P	Full House	7	17	7	80	11.43
WACH–TV	M–F	1030P	Arsenio Hall	7	15	8	80	10.00
				63	145	89	$785	

[a]Note that two commercials per week were purchased in Regis/Kathy Lee.

Number of stations used: 3   Total GRPs/week: 63
Daytime GRPs/week: 30   Fringe GRPs/week: 33
Total women impressions: 145,000   Women 25–54 impressions: 89,000
CPM women 25–54 impressions: $8.82   Weekly cost: $785

Note: CPM women aged 25–54 impressions is calculated by dividing the weekly cost times 1,000 by the total women aged 25–54 impressions.

$$\frac{785 \times 1,000}{89,000} = 8.82$$

Developing a Regional Media Plan

How to Use This Assignment

You will want to use this assignment as a take-home assignment, to give students the opportunity to evaluate media alternatives and costs. Students will also need time to prepare the written media plan.

What to Emphasize in Class

Students should review the problem for all available clues. The media planner who works on small, regional accounts often has less detailed information than planners who work on large, national accounts. Common sense and logic will be needed to supplement the lack of available data.

Advise students to carefully review Assignment 26, "Writing Media Objectives," and Assignment 28, "Media Plan Checklist," before they begin writing their media plans. If you have not used Assignments 27 or 29 on planning media strategies, this would be a good time to review one or both in class so students have a better idea of what is required and how strategies differ from objectives.

Note: You or your students may notice that the audience and cost figures used in this assignment differ slightly from those shown elsewhere in the workbook. This is because they came from a different source. This is not an unusual circumstance in advertising where some agencies and clients prefer one source for spot TV cost data and others choose another. In any case, the figures are similar, and students should use the data provided in this assignment.

Answer to Problem for Assignment 35

What follows is a solution to the media planning problem posed by this assignment. Keep in mind that there is no single correct answer to such a complex assignment. Different planners will have different approaches to the problem. The things to look for in student plans are the logic and appropriateness of their answers and the rationale they have provided to support their recommendations.

Media Objectives

1. **Target audience.** To the extent possible, target messages toward female homemakers aged 35+ living in metropolitan markets.

2. **Coverage/regionality.** Provide media coverage in all the ADIs in the North and South Carolina marketing area. (This is certainly called for by the marketing objectives. There are no indications in the background information that any ADIs are to be given extra weight.)

3. **Seasonality/scheduling.** Plan to start advertising at the beginning of the second quarter of the year (April) and run through the higher usage months of April through September. Provide added weight during the first six

115

weeks of the campaign. (The budget will not permit year-long advertising at adequate weight levels. The decision was made to lead the season by starting in April to get a jump on competition. Another planner might have waited until May to launch the campaign. The added weight during the first six weeks is certainly appropriate based on the marketing objectives.)

4. **Reach/frequency.** To the extent possible, within budget constraints, select media that enhance reach to target audience consumers. This is especially important during the introductory period. (This is a difficult assignment given the modest budget, but it is certainly a worthwhile goal based on the marketing background and communications objectives.)

5. **Creative implications.** Use media that provide visualization to help quickly establish package and brand identity. (Given the need to quickly build brand awareness, visualization seems a logical media attribute.)

6. **Promotion support.** Provide media to support a coupon promotion at the kick-off of the campaign. (Although not specifically required of the media plan, this objective is certainly merited based on the creative/promotion background statement and on the advertising/communications objectives.)

7. **Merchandisability.** To the extent possible, use media that are merchandisable to the retail trade. (An important consideration in light of the marketing and advertising objectives related to building retail awareness and cooperation.)

8. **Budget.** Accomplish the foregoing objectives within a working media budget of $300,000.

Media Strategies

1. Use half-page, four-color ads in regional editions of magazines to provide a carrier for coupons at the campaign kick-off and to provide a strong visual image for the brand. Magazine ads supporting the brand will provide some prestige and will help offset any negative connotations associated with a regional brand. Proofs of the four-color print ads will also be of value in merchandising the advertising to the retail trade.

2. Use spot TV in key ADIs in the two-state marketing area to dramatically promote the product. Use a combination of prime and fringe dayparts during the kick-off period to build initial reach, then use fringe only during the latter stages of the campaign. Prime and/or fringe dayparts will generate higher reach than daytime. Additionally, spot television in those dayparts is very merchandisable to the retail trade.

3. Run the heaviest advertising weight during the months of April and May to kick off the campaign, then reduce advertising for the rest of the summer selling season (June through September).

Media Selections/Rationale

Magazines. Only two regional magazines were available. These were the only ones providing state-by-state regional breakouts. Regional editions of other magazines included too much waste circulation. Both magazines were used in order to generate additional reach, even though they are not equally efficient in terms of cost per thousand. Only two insertions are scheduled in each magazine, and the lack of efficiency has been offset by the greater reach provided by the combination. It is estimated that the two magazines will generate a reach of 20 percent as opposed to about 10–11 percent for either one used alone.

If more regional editions had been available or if more extensive schedules had been planned, greater emphasis would have been placed on selecting those magazines with the best cost efficiency. In consideration of the budget constraint, half pages were used to keep costs down. While one-third pages could have been used in *Southern Living,* any savings would have been offset by the additional production costs needed to produce ads in two different sizes.

Spot television. Spot television was selected because of its dynamic nature. Equal weight is scheduled for all markets. There is nothing in the marketing background that would justify varying weights by market. For three weeks during the first month of the campaign, 35 GRPs in prime and 40 GRPs in fringe are recommended. This combination, when combined with the 19 percent magazine reach, will generate a combined reach of 77 percent for the kick-off month of April.

Newspapers. Newspapers were not recommended because of the high cost for even small (20-inch) ads and the lack of color. A single 20-inch, black-and-white ad in all the newspapers would have cost $14,349. Newspaper ads equivalent to a half page (60 inches) would cost $43,046 per insertion.

Spot radio. Spot radio was not used because it lacks the visual appeal of television. Also, daytime spot radio costs were only marginally less than for fringe time television. A possible variation would be to combine prime-time television with spot radio, but this does not appear as feasible as the recommended plan, given the budget constraints that would severely limit the amount of prime-time television that could be purchased.

Scheduling

As shown on the scheduling chart, advertising is concentrated in the April–September period, with the heaviest weight in the April–May kick-off period. This scheduling is consistent with the marketing and advertising objectives. However, another planner might vary the length of the heavy-up period or the specific number of GRPs per week. Any attempt to spread the advertising over a longer period, however, would result in very low reach and frequency levels.

The reach and frequency figures for spot TV were estimated from the spot television reach table in Assignment 16. Monthly magazine reach was estimated by taking circulation as a percentage of the TV households in the two-state area. TV households were used because that figure was given in the ADI listing in the assignment. Because TV penetration is over 98 percent, the resulting reach estimates are reasonably accurate. The figures would not vary much even if total households were known and used. Spot TV reaches for different dayparts and magazine reaches were combined using the Sainsbury formula as discussed in Assignment 17.

Budget Recap

Medium	Total Cost	Percentage of Total
Magazines	$ 45,718	15%
Spot television	250,675	85
	$296,393	100%

Magazines

Better Homes & Gardens—1/2 pg., 4/c—2 @ 9,779 . . . . $19,558
Southern Living—1/2 pg., 4/c—2 @ 13,080   26,160

Spot television

Market	Prime C/RP	Fringe C/RP
Charlotte	117	42
Raleigh–Durham	135	63
Greenville–Spartanburg–Asheville	80	39
Greensboro–Winston Salem	94	35
Columbia	46	20
Charleston	39	16
	511	215

Prime—5 weeks @ 35 GRPs = 175 GRPs @ 511   89,425
Fringe—5 weeks @ 40 and 11 weeks @ 50 GRPs =
  750 GRPs @ 215. 161,250
    Total $250,675

Spot Television Cost per Market

Market	Cost prime	Cost fringe	Total cost
Charlotte	$20,475	$31,500	$51,975
Raleigh–Durham	23,625	47,250	70,875
Greenville–Spartanburg–Asheville	14,000	29,250	43,250
Greensboro–Winston Salem	16,450	26,250	42,700
Columbia	8,050	15,000	23,050
Charleston	6,825	12,000	18,825
	$89,425	$161,250	$250,675

Exhibit 35–1 Advertising Flowchart

	Jan.	Feb.	Mar.	Apr.	May	June	July	Aug.	Sept.	Oct.	Nov.	Dec.	Total
MAGAZINES 1/2 PG. 4/C													
B H & G				■	■								
SO. LIVING					■								
SPOT TV													
PRIME 35 GRP						■	■	■	■				
FRINGE 40 GRP													
FRINGE 50 GRP													
Monthly REACH				65	76	53	48	35	35				
Monthly FREQUENCY				2.6	3.2	3.8	3.1	2.9	2.9				
Dollars per mo.(000)				75.8	102.3	43.0	32.3	21.5	21.5				296.4
Budget monthly(%)				25.6	34.5	14.5	10.9	7.3	7.3				100.0

Evaluating a Media Plan

How to Use This Assignment

This is an assignment that could be done by each student in class, or as part of a final paper on the subject. The goal is to provoke thought about how to evaluate a media plan. It might be a good idea to have students think about the problem, if they do not write a paper on it, and bring their notes to class in order to discuss the subject.

What to Emphasize in Class

The most important aspect of this topic is that we, in the industry, do not have a foolproof way of evaluating a media plan. Of course, we have criteria, and one goal of the assignment is to see whether students know these criteria. But that does not change the situation. We do not know how to evaluate a media plan in an objective manner.

Nevertheless, we have selected what we think are the most important criteria and those that we know many other expert media planners would also choose. However, students might be able to add additional criteria. If their criteria are reasonable, students will have learned some standards that are important in media planning.

Answer to Problem for Assignment 36

The reasons that each criterion listed is important in media planning follow:

1. **Media objectives.** These grow out of marketing objectives and strategies. A media planner who ignores marketing is not logical. Furthermore, a media plan is supposed to fulfill goals. Without goals we spend advertising dollars aimlessly.

2. **Media strategies (and tactics).** Nothing is as important as strategies. These are means to the goals. But note that they are not any means; they are the *best of all alternatives*. A poor strategy does not lead to the goals, except accidentally.

3. **Reach/frequency/GRP.** The summation of a media plan is expressed in these terms (i.e., R/F/GRP equal delivery of targets in certain patterns). A media plan that does not prove its delivery cannot assess its success. R/F/GRP are also useful for comparative purposes with other media plans. One therefore can learn by comparison and contrast.

4. **Media vehicle selection.** This criterion is obvious, but it includes objective and subjective choices. It includes CPM, appropriateness of vehicles for certain products, and proof that vehicles reach a large number of targets.

5. **Weighting geographically.** There are no national markets where each market is of equal value to every other. That being the case, a planner

should spend more or place more GRPs in the best potential markets for sales. It would be foolish to do otherwise.

6. **Timing and scheduling.** An old advertising and selling axiom is: Sell the right product to the right people at the right time. What is the right time? "When people are buying!" One should rarely advertise in poor sales months in hopes of building markets. The history of such attempts is full of failures.

7. **Spending plan.** When large amounts of money are to be spent, it is prudent to plan such expenditures carefully. The more thorough the analysis of spending, the better one can control it. A reasonable spending plan is a necessity. Also, planners cannot spend more than their clients allow.

8. **Creative strategy input.** One should never plan media without first checking the creative plan. In fact, this criterion should be placed before all other criteria. Other criteria might be more important, but creative strategy directly influences media strategy.

9. **Calculations and accuracy.** Incorrect calculations can nullify strategy. Small rounding errors are insignificant. But large errors mean that planners have not done what they said they were going to do.

10. **Innovativeness of the plan.** Many a media plan looks exactly like everyone else's media plan. Is it possible to achieve a plan's goals in a truly innovative way? If so, one *might* have a better plan. But a wise planner is not confused with plans that are called "creative" but have no reasoned discipline about them; one *must* be creative within a logical framework. Such a plan could achieve significant goals for the client.

11. **Mechanical structure and communicability of the plan.** No matter how good an idea a planner has, it will lose its effectiveness if no one understands it. The planner must help everyone understand a plan. This means good organization, good headings and subheadings, and, most important, good, easy-to-understand tables and graphs. All of this tends to be mechanical, but it is very important.